To Jim,

Ye Great Editor.

Thanks for another job
Well done!

Penny + Jerry greatly appreciate
your help.

Best Regards,

Joseph Webb

Alex – A Lesson in Courage
Copyright © 2019 Joseph W. Bebo
Published by Joseph W. Bebo
(An imprint of J.W.M. Bebo Books Publishing)

This is a work of nonfiction. All the people and events mentioned in the book are real.

Joseph W. Bebo
PO Box 762
Hudson, MA, 01749
Email: joewbebobooks@gmail.com
Editors: James Oliveri and Yvonne Miloyevich
Cover Design: Jerry and Penny Gentile, and Elyse Zielinski

Library of Congress Cataloging in – Publication Data
Joseph W. Bebo
Alex – A Lesson in Courage /Joseph Bebo – First Edition

ISBN: 978-1-7339308-0-2

Non-fiction, biography; Special Needs

Alex

A Lesson In Courage

Joseph W. Bebo

This book is dedicated to Penny, Jerry, and Alex Gentile.

Preface

Alex was special in many ways. He wasn't given much to start his life with. He couldn't talk or walk, and it was doubtful he would develop much beyond a nine-month-old child, but Alex's disabilities didn't define him. He not only had special needs, he had special parents, an exceptional school system with dedicated teachers, and an extraordinary support environment in a unique city. I will be using these words repeatedly in the following story, but what transpired is extraordinary by every definition of that term. Alex not only interacted with hundreds of people, he touched them and taught them about life.

Courage isn't always something you go into battle with beforehand. Many heroes don't think of themselves as courageous. It often springs up unaware in the hour of dire need and isn't noticed until everything is over. You did what you had to do. That kind of courage is what this book is about. It's a story about a little boy and his parents that shows what love can overcome to turn a seeming tragedy into a wondrous joy.

Chapter 1 – The Medium

July 7, 2018

The Medium - "Your father just came in, Jerry. He's very proud of you. You're living in the same house you grew up in, aren't you? Penny, you have three siblings who are living. Your father is concerned that you feel as if you are in a cloud. These are troubled times. You've had a recent loss. He wants to help you.

"Jerry, your mother is here. She says the maintenance of the house is too much. Keep it simple. You aren't puttering around anymore. Plant flowers. Get some planters and grow flowers. You need to get out of the house to feel better.

"You have a pool in the backyard. Get out of the house, find some projects. Get out with nature."

(A long silence)

(The only thing the medium knew was their first names)

"Your mothers are coming through from the other side. They are very proud of you. Penny, your mother will stay with you, to lift your heart out of depression. Thank you for being so patient with Jerry.

"Have faith, God will hear your prayers. Going to church will help. Surround yourself with good feelings and people who will be helpful for you."

Jerry – "Is there anything about Alex?"

The Medium – "Yes, Alex is here. Ask him to come closer. Your son?

(Sound of sobbing)

"Alex says he's so sorry. Penny, you're picking up everyone. He holds your hand when you're in bed, and sees you awake. He tries to give you peace.

(When Alex and Penny slept together, he would always hold her hand.)

"He has a charismatic personality. He was loved and joyful and happy. I can feel his happiness. He can express himself. I can feel that love."

Jerry – "Alex couldn't talk."

(A long silence)

(Birds singing softly outside)

Medium - "He had a different way of walking. A limp? He knew everybody loved him. He made everybody smile. He was having dental work? More than just a cleaning. It didn't happen.

"He loved animals. He could get loud. He was very friendly. He thanks you for your dedication. You gave up things and sacrificed for him. He needed constant attention. You are just amazing parents and deserve much praise. He had a routine. Penny made it fun.

"You had to pick him up. You never felt that taking care of him was a job. It was just something you loved to do. Things had to be a certain way or he wouldn't like it. You respected that. Thank you."

Jerry – "Can you tell us what happened?"

The Medium – "You have a ramp in front of your house. It made it so much easier for him. I see a bubble. Alex could interact with people. He could grab you and pull you and direct you. You stopped what you were doing whenever he wanted you. He is so very grateful. He wasn't able to express himself. He didn't like taking a bath. He says this will make Mommy laugh. He's sorry about that.

"He's referencing his head. There's ringing in his ears. His head hurts. The ringing is uncomfortable. He has a tough time swallowing. Not able to swallow…ringing in his ears…disorienting…breathing.

"I'm seeing water, pressure in his head. There was a rapid decline. You weren't supposed to find him. He's sorry for that."

Penny – "Did he try to come to us before he died?"

The Medium – "He knew he wasn't feeling well, but he couldn't. There was a ceremony in the school in his honor? Outdoors in the field with other kids, a great success. He was very excited. He was happy. He felt included.

"He loved driving in the car. He loved to go for rides. Such a beautiful soul."

Jerry – "Why did he go?"

The Medium – "Seizures. He wasn't able to come to you. He was paralyzed with shaking episodes, more than you were aware of. It was exhausting for him. You weren't supposed to be there that night. Had you been there, it wouldn't have changed anything."

Penny – "Tell him we miss him."

Medium – "Talk to him out loud, he will come and be with you. Don't be so angry. It's time to clean things out. Get rid of the wheelchair. Donate it. You are both stronger than you think you are. He was a magnet for joy. Your parents will be with you. Talk to Alex as you water the flowers."

"He wants Penny to be involved with Special Olympics. Be open, a lot of good comes from that. Alex says that there was so much love in his home. You're not sleeping well. You will see Alex in your dreams. You will have a visitation, but you must sleep peacefully before this can happen.

"Alex loves music, so play music for him. You can do this. He'll help you. You have a great support network with family and friends. You have a wonderful neighborhood, he's telling me, and all of those loved ones on the other-side. They're all together and happy.

"Jerry, you were a good advocate. He is with you in many ways. You have tons of pictures of him. There was a lot of support at school. Thank Barbara for him.

"He thanks you for taking care of his friend."

Jerry – "What friend?"

(The medium cannot come up with the name, but said she did this certain thing. Penny immediately knew who she was taking about!)

Medium - "The pain made him tired. He was tired. Sleep apnia was part of it, but it was more the accumulative effect of the seizures. He had a very happy life and is very grateful."

Penny – "Tell him we love him and miss him and want to be with him."

Chapter 2 – Beginnings

Penny Randazza (christened Marguerite) and Jerry Gentile (christened Gerald) met at the Malden Trust Bank, in Malden, Massachusetts, where they both worked.

"I liked his voice," Penny told me.

According to Cindy Kelloway, a long time friend who worked with them at the bank, Jerry adored Penny.

Jerry was born on August 2, 1956, Penny on April 26, 1962.

They were a nice couple, perfect for each other, but there was certainly nothing heroic about them, at least not to the eye.

They got married a few years after meeting, in late 1987. Jerry, who was born in Woburn, Mass., had lived in Malden most of his life, in the same house they now live in. Penny was born and grew up in Charlestown, where she lived in the project for the first few years of her life. She had nine brothers and sisters. Jerry was an only child. His father was of Italian descent. His mother was French-Canadian. Penny's father was Italian and her mother, Irish.

Penny's brother, Jimmy, and sister, Marlene, were both older than her by several years, more babysitters to her than siblings. Marlene remembers Penny as being their dad's favorite and spoiled. Penny had two other siblings, a brother, Joey, who was a year older, and a sister, Paula, who was two years younger.

Penny also had several older siblings she never really knew, severely disabled children, who had either died before she was born or soon after. Of these children, four in all, one was institutionalized in a hospital, while the others were kept at home and cared for by their mother, who didn't work. None of them went to school.

Her brother, Joey, and sister, Paula, were Penny's playmates. She didn't know Paula had special needs. To Penny, growing up, she was just her playmate. Then one day, Paula, too, was gone.

Marlene, Penny's older sister - "We had four Special Needs kids in our family. None of them went to school. One was institutionalized. One, who's name was Paula, was two years younger than Penny. She had cerebral palsy, bad, and couldn't walk or talk. My mother took care of her. Paula died when she was fourteen."

Marlene remembered that Paula was never made part of the family, but Penny remembers playing with her on the stoop together when they were kids.

Marlene felt bad for her parents because of her sisters.

"They had a hard life. Dad worked two or three jobs to support the family. Mothers did not work then."

Jimmy, Penny's older brother - "We had four special needs children (sisters) in our family. Nancy, who was completely disabled and had to be fed and changed, Marian, who could walk with braces, Theresa, who died young, and Paula, who could sit up, but never walked or talked. Our parents had to do everything for them. Me, too."

Marlene doesn't believe Alex's condition was hereditary, because his was so different from her siblings. They all had much to learn about just how special Alex was.

Penny, who was living at home before she married Jerry, always worried she might have a child like her mother, but wanted children nonetheless. Her brother, Jimmy, had a family of his own[1], none of which had shown a problem.

Jerry's dad died the year after they were married, on October 31, 1988. His mother, Esther, lived alone in the family home, and was very supportive. Penny's mother, Margaret, and Father, Randy or Reggio, still lived in Charlestown, and were already proud grandparents, who doted on their grandkids. Penny and Jerry would have a strong family support system. They would need it.

Cindy Kelloway, long-time friend – "Penny was surrounded by the children of family and friends, especially among the people she worked with at the bank. We were always going to their christenings and birthday parties."

Penny wanted nothing more than to have a child of her own. Finding she was having difficulties conceiving, she finally tried intrauterine insemination. It worked. Penny became pregnant.

They were living in a second story apartment in Everett at the time. Friends and family rejoiced, but that joy was short-lived when Penny had a miscarriage and lost the baby. It was a very sad time for everyone, but especially for Penny and Jerry. She had prayed so hard and had so much hope, but she didn't give up or get discouraged, and was soon pregnant again.

---

[1] Jimmy has two grown boys, Jimmy and Jeff, and a girl, Elaine, and six grandkids.

Unfortunately, once again, bad news soon followed. After a visit to the clinic they learned the child had spinal bifida, a very serious condition, where there is an opening in the spine. This could lead to damage of the spinal cord and nerves that send messages to and from the brain, which could result in any number of severe disabilities, including paralysis and the inability to walk or talk, etc. Following the advice of doctors, family, and friends, they decided to end the pregnancy, something Penny regrets to this day. She objected, but everyone told her it would be cruel and irresponsible to knowingly bring a child with such handicaps and needs into the world to suffer a life of unhappiness and neglect.

If they only knew what they know now.

Things were pretty low after that. Even Penny's strong determination and resilience were tested, but still they did not give up. Then one day a miracle occurred. Her prayers were answered.

Chapter 3 – The Arrival

Alex was born at 6:40 pm, on September 26, 1996.

**Penny's Journal -To Our Baby Boy, Who is going to be Born Today!
(1996) Thursday, Sept. 26**

It's Thursday, September 26, 1996. It's 6:30 am and Daddy is taking Mommy to Melrose Wakefield Hospital to wait the delivery of our baby.

At 6:40 pm our baby boy was born, weighing in at 8 lbs, 2 oz, and 20 ins long, by C-Section, your daddy watched the birth.

After you were born, everyone was there waiting to see you – Grammy, Nana and Papa, Uncle Joey and Uncle Jim, whose birthday is the same day as yours. Auntie Mary asks what your name is and Daddy answers, "Alexander". Your cousins Jeff and Elaine Marie were there too.

At 9:12 pm a lunar eclipse began, and at 9:45 pm the nursery nurse brought you to see Mommy and Daddy, and you're beautiful! You have dark brown hair and brown eyes. You look just like your daddy.

The baby appeared to be a normal, healthy baby boy. Penny was in labor for twelve hours and in the end delivered by C-section. When someone asked, "What's his name?" Penny answered, jokingly, "Pooh," but Jerry announced, "Alexander."[2]

Penny's oldest brother, Jimmy - "Alex was born the same day I was. He was my first nephew. I looked outside and it was a beautiful night with a bright full moon. I thought it was a special night – fitting since my first nephew and I had the same birthday. He seemed normal when we first saw him. He was wrapped in a little blanket. There was nothing unusual, except for the lunar eclipse. We went home and next day Penny called and said they found an issue."

The next day Jerry noticed that the baby seemed to be perspiring profusely.

"Why is he sweating so much?" he asked.

The doctor took one look at Alex and immediately ordered an ambulance to take him to the Natal Care Unit at Children's Hospital in Boston, where he was placed in Intensive Care. Alex would be there for the next month.

---

[2] Jerry isn't sure where the name came from, but his grandfather's name was an Italian form of the name, Alexander.

Penny's Journal – Friday, Sept. 27

You had to be transferred to Children's Hospital in Boston today. You were having a little problem. The doctors at Melrose Wakefield sent you to the best hospital so you could get better and come home to Mommy and Daddy. Daddy and Auntie Marlene stayed with you the whole day and Daddy was there all the time to make sure you were OK.

It turned out that Alex had an enlarged heart, liver, and spleen, as well as low blood-sugar and low oxygen in his blood. It was a very critical situation. Penny was alarmed when they told her the news. She was in her hospital room recovering from the C-section. She called Jerry, who had gone home to wait for news on Alex after he had been taken to Children's Hospital. On hearing the news, he went right over and stayed there with Marlene, Penny's sister, to be with his new born son. Alex had an IV tube in his arm and a feeding tube down his throat, as well as an oxygen hose taped over his nose. When Penny saw him two days later, after leaving the hospital, she was shocked. He looked so small and helpless.

The doctors could tell them little, except that they would have to wait and see what happened. So they waited and watched. For three days, Penny and Jerry never left Alex's side. Each day after that, Penny would go in to be with Alex, while Jerry went to work. At the end of the day, Jerry would come and sit with Penny until five or six, then they would go home to dinner. They'd return at seven to stay with the child until mid-night, sometimes one in the morning. Penny would sleep at Jerry's mother's house so she would be closer to the hospital. They did this every day for a month.

Slowly, over time, as the doctors watched and marveled, each condition corrected itself. It was a scary, distressing time for Penny and Jerry, but they trusted the doctors, who they believed were giving Alex the best treatment possible. Luckily, after a month, Alex was able to leave the hospital. Penny and Jerry were overjoyed.

Friends and family were all concerned when they learned about the difficulty Penny and Jerry were having with their baby. Everyone knew how much this child meant to them and the troubles she'd had previously. They hoped it was not happening again. You can imagine everyone's relief and joy when they heard that their prayers had been answered and Alex had recovered.

Alex left Children's Hospital on October 8th and went to the Melrose Wakefield Hospital Natal Care Unit to learn how to take a bottle and eat.

Finally, Penny and Jerry had their child, a normal, now healthy, baby boy. Each day at Melrose-Wakefield, Alex progressed as expected. His pediatrician, Dr. Masucci, said he would soon be ready to go home. The big event occurred when Gilda, his nurse, found a bottle-nipple that was really easy for Alex to drink from. This little victory had everyone jumping and clapping for joy, for it meant Alex would be coming home.

Penny's Journal – October 13
Alex comes home to Mommy and Daddy!

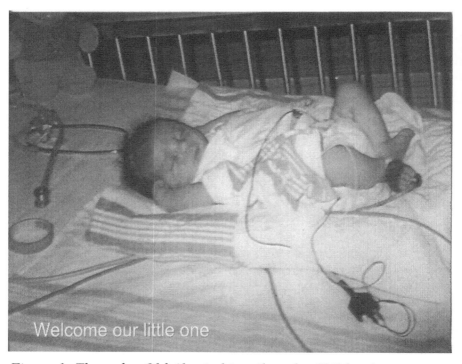

Figure 1- Three day Old Alex in his crib at the Children's Hospital Natal ICU

Jerry's mother, Esther, who was called Grammy, called the baby, 'Darling'. Penny's father, who they called Papa, called him, 'My Little Devil'. Alex soon became the center of attention.

That Halloween, Penny and Jerry took him out trick-or-treating dressed as 'Winnie the Pooh', the first of many costumes Alex would don. Winnie the Pooh would become one of Alex's favorite animal characters. He visited Penny's parents, and Jerry's mother, as well as his Uncle Jim, Penny's oldest brother, who was at the hospital with his wife when Alex was born.

Alex was christened on November 10. They had a big party at their apartment in Everett.

A month later, Alex went to Jerry's work party, where the gang at the bank met him for the first time. These were the first of many excursions Alex would go on. Alex was being introduced to the world.

They took him everywhere, the proud new parents showing off their child. Some of Jerry's friends suspected that this would be the end of his concert-going days. He assured them it would not, although he did cut back a bit.

That Christmas Penny, Jerry, and Alex made the rounds to the various relatives.

Penny's Journal – December 25
Alex's First Christmas. Nana and Papa, Auntie and Uncle Joe, Uncle Joey and Auntie Kim, are here to watch me open all my presents. Mommy helps me. Then off to Grammy's house to open more presents, then we travel to Uncle Jim and Auntie Mary's house. Alex got tons of presents!

Penny's and Jerry's dream had come true. They were finally parents. Alex was everything they had dreamed of and prayed for. One of the first things they discovered about their new baby boy was his smile.

(1997) Penny's Journal – January 4
Alexander leaves Mommy and Daddy's room to sleep in his crib. Daddy wasn't ready for this. He wanted you to stay in the bassinet. He was even going to sleep on the floor next to you. But guess what, you slept all night and in the morning you gave Daddy and Mommy a big smile.

Alex appeared to be developing normally. At three months he was turning over from his stomach to his back and back again, and was crawling along the floor. Best of all, he was smiling. He didn't keep them up all night crying. He was the perfect baby.

That Easter he was again brought to see all the relatives, Grammy, Nana and Papa, Uncle Jimmy and Joey and their families. Alex was the center of attention. Easter baskets full of candy and money were given out. Penny's family was extremely pleased for her and took the baby into their hearts.

Alex continued to develop, hitting all his goals. He ate cereal for the first time. He got his first tooth. He discovered his toes and put them in his mouth, and never left his socks on. Everyday was a new discovery and entered in Penny's journal. Then suddenly, at six months old, a dark cloud appeared on the horizon. Alex was still not able to sit up on his own. He started missing his goals and was not developing as expected.

Still life went on.

On Father's Day, that June, Penny, Jerry, and Alex went out to dinner, the first of many such repasts. The next day they went to the park, where Alex went on the swings and sat on the slide. They noticed he seemed to be weak and not able to do things on his own other children his age could do.

In the beginning of July 1997, the family took Alex on vacation with them to Maine, where Alex sat in a beach chair, listening to the waves. He was enthralled by the water flowing under him. It was a magical time.

Two weeks later, nine months and twenty-something days after his birth, Alex's parents took him to the Children's Hospital in Boston for some tests. There, an MRI found a problem. Alex's brain was not developing normally.

Chapter 4 – Early Intervention

Penny and Jerry were alarmed to learn about Alex's condition, although they didn't get a lot of specific information. Things were vague. They were given different diagnoses by different doctors at different times. It was understandable. No one knew much about Alex's condition. There was hardly anything written about it in the medical books at the time.

In spite of the disturbing news, they found that Alex was easy to care for and had a good disposition. He had his own personality. Penny loved to hold him and fought with Jerry's mother over who would take him. Jerry's mother, Esther, was a major source of support during Alex's early years, taking care of him so that Penny could work and help pay the mounting bills. 'Grammy' loved the boy and accepted him fully into her life, knowing the difficulty a Special Needs child like Alex could entail. She not only supported them emotionally and practically, but financially as well.

Cindy Kelloway, a close and long time friend – "Esther was a Godsend and loved by all who knew her."

Alex couldn't be left alone, but Esther was there through the early years. She wanted him with her at her house all the time. Penny would go to work and leave Alex with Jerry's mom all day. She loved him, even purchasing life-insurance for him at an early age. She knew what they were up against. Unfortunately, she had Lupus, and died unexpectedly in 2001 of complications from the disease.

Like any child, Alex was a very affectionate baby and showed his love. He would smile up at them and laugh when they tickled him. Everyone agreed that he had a great smile. He was well formed, with regular features and no obvious physical defects. He was a good looking kid.

He seemed to be enjoying himself as he cruised around the floor, crawling and holding on to things to move about. Sometimes something would get his attention and he would smile or laugh. Alex didn't cry and didn't have tantrums. He had a happy, pleasant disposition.

Penny and Jerry may have been uncertain about many things, but not about their child. He had become the one certain thing in their lives. They loved him with all their hearts.

As much attention as Penny and Jerry got in doctors' offices and hospitals, so far they had been entirely on their own, with only Penny's family and Jerry's mother for support. That all changed after one of their visits to the Children's Hospital.

They were there to see Alex's neurologist, who, although he couldn't give them a complete diagnosis, tried to give them hope. They were leaving, feeling a bit dejected, when a nurse noticed that Alex, who was nine months old, could not sit up. She talked to them for a while, and then gave Penny and Jerry a number to call for state assistance.

Penny's Journal – July, 1997

Alex is starting an early intervention program. This will help Alex to get strong and help him catch up. Alex has many people to help him. Sandra is his physical therapist, who sees him three times a week.

Right from the beginning, Jerry and Penny had to deal with well-meaning doctors, who, having no idea of Alex's real condition, treated him like so many other children with better-known needs. And right from the beginning, Penny and Jerry fought against this. Alex was special.

The experts at Early Intervention ran a series of tests, trying to make him do things Alex would never be able to do because of his severe brain developmental issue. They finally told Penny that Alex was retarded. Penny gave them a few choice words and walked out.

Even though this may seem like an insensitive, callous way to explain to Penny and Jerry their child's special needs, it goes to show how little even the experts knew about Alex's condition at the time. They would all soon learn. Alex would teach them.

His parents knew Alex would never be like other children, and wished the experts could recognize the differences and help them deal with his specific needs. Their persistent complaints and determination led to changes in the program, as experts and caregivers began to recognize Alex's unique requirements, but it took time.

The Shore Collaborative Early Intervention Program was a state funded service for physical, occupational, and speech therapy. Alex remained in the program for the next two and half years, until he turned three, learning how to communicate.

In September, Penny took Alex to his first day at the Play Group, which met every Wednesday, where he sang songs and played with the other children. Play Group was part of Early Intervention and one of four separate activities: Mommy and Me, where the mother and child played together; Magenta Group, oriented to sensory activity, where Penny also worked with Alex; and Blue Group, where Alex worked without his mother. As Penny records in her Journal, Kathy and Mary Lou were the teachers, there to help him learn, and Ann, the service coordinator, made sure everything went right. They played with Jell-O, oatmeal, and noodles, and climbed over obstacles to build their strength and dexterity.

This was Alex's and his parents' first foray into a world of support formed by the city and state coming into existence at just this time for the aid of Special Needs children and their families. It was a net that was to help sustain them for the rest of Alex's life, and which will form much of the subject of this story.

One of Penny's best friends is Mary Gasdia.

"I've known Penny for twenty-two years, since fall of 1997."

They met in Play Group in Early Intervention.

"My second daughter, Nicole, was born three months prematurely. She weighed two pounds, and needed the early intervention program to help her catch up developmentally. Penny and I both lived in Malden and were stay-at-home moms. I thought Penny was very caring. I gravitated to her. We were sounding boards for each other and shared information."

Her daughter, Nicole, is now twenty-two, the same age as Alex. Mary has another daughter, Carianna, who is twenty-three.

Mary – "When my daughter caught up developmentally after a few months, she joined the mainstream classes. We moved to Wakefield when Nicole was in second grade and joined that city's public school system, but I stayed friends with Penny."

Nicole moved through the grades along with all the other typical kids, graduating from high school in 2015. She has gone on to college and will graduate in May of 2019 with a Radiology Technician's degree. Although she developed normally, Nicole still has health issues, probably as a result of her premature birth.

Mary – "Alex was lucky. He wanted for nothing and experienced everything. They never complained. Other moms at Early Intervention would cry and complain, 'Why me?', 'I can't go out', 'I'm stuck with the kid eight hours a day until my husband comes home'. Penny never did that." (Just the opposite).

It was about this time that Alex had his first visit with Dr. Millis, an orthopedic physician, who was to follow his bone development. Soon after that, he was fitted for his first pair of leg braces to help strengthen his legs and ankles. He learned to combat crawl.

Still, no one could give them a definitive explanation of their son's condition.

Chapter 5 – The Diagnosis

The challenges that faced Alex and his parents were many, and some might have found them overwhelming, but Penny and Jerry seemed not to notice. Their lives went on as usual. They both continued to work, and Jerry continued to go to concerts – much to the surprise of many of his friends. Little things like this, a night out with his friends listening to music, probably helped sustain him and remind him of more carefree days.

They continued to take care of Alex, bringing him everywhere.

On his first birthday they had a big party for him at the apartment. All his family, friends, and neighbors came. It would be the first of many such parties, which were always lavish events.

Penny's Journal, Sept 26, 1997
> Alex's First Birthday. Mommy and Daddy have a big party with a Winnie the Pooh cake and all your relatives and friends come celebrate with you.

Alex continued to progress through the Early Intervention Program, which sent therapists and paras[3] to the home to continue therapy.

Then, in early October, Alex had another MRI at the Children's Hospital. A few weeks later, during a visit to Dr. Urion, his neurologist, they learned that Alex had an undeveloped Vermis[4], as well as low myelination[5]. He told them that Alex's development would be slow and that he would have low muscle tone. This was the first definitive

---

[3] Para means 'next to' or 'assistant'. It is a person who assists in a Special Ed classroom. They help watch the children and have training in how to care for their special needs.

[4] The Vermis is the middle lobe connecting the two halves of the brain. It controls communication between the Right and Left Hemispheres of the brain. This communication is vital to the full, proper functioning of the organ (some say the key to intelligence).

[5] Myelination is the formation of Myelin around axons of the neurons in the brain. Myelin is a sheath or fatty-coating around our nerves, which protects them and allows nerve impulses to move more freely. Myelination begins in the brain stem and cerebellum before birth, but not in the frontal cortex until later in adolescence.

diagnosis they had to date, but still, there was much they did not know and which no one could tell them.

Penny and Jerry did not panic or become dejected. They took one day at a time, determined to do whatever they needed to take care of their child. They never thought of it as hard or tragic. At no time did they feel bad or sorry for themselves. They simply gave him all their love.

Their only concern was for their boy, although they were being told some pretty scary things, things that would have made many consider their options, but not Penny and Jerry. When they looked at Alex they saw a little bundle of joy and delight. Their happiness at having a child outweighed all other considerations.

Marlene, Penny's sister – "Everyone was excited and happy for Penny that first year. We all thought Alex was a normal baby. At some point Penny learned the stem of Alex's brain wasn't connected, and he wouldn't be able to do anything for himself, he'd be a perpetually helpless baby. We were heartbroken, but I was very impressed with how Penny and Jerry handled it."

When Jimmy found out that Alex's brain stem wasn't developed and he wouldn't be able to do anything for himself, he also felt heartbroken for them.

"I knew how hard it would be after seeing my parents go through it. It took all their energy and time. For thirty years, with Special Needs children, they never went anywhere. Only after the last one died, did they finally start to go out again."

Penny and Jerry were never given a definitive prognosis. No one seemed to know how far he would develop, if at all, only that his development would be slow. They were told that if he didn't walk by five years old, he never would. They did not lose heart. They simply continued to do what they had been doing for the past nine-months, take care of Alex.

His parents maintain that they were never told that Alex wouldn't develop beyond the level of a helpless baby, although Penny's brother and sister seem to believe this to be the case. No one knew for sure. In any event, none of this mattered. There was no way they were going to give up on their child. Institutionalization was never an option for them.

Penny's brother, Jimmy – "They tested him for a couple of years. They were told he'd never walk or talk or be able to interact with people. He walked up the ramp to get his high school diploma, and he interacted with people big time. Penny and Jerry met it head on."

Penny – "Alex hadn't asked to be brought into the world. We brought him into it."

Jerry – "We decided to give our lives to Alex. Everything we would do, we would do with Alex."

As we shall see, they would take him everywhere.

Still, no one could tell Penny and Jerry why this had happened. Was it hereditary? Was it something they did? Or was it one of those things that just happen? It was a mystery that lasted fourteen years.

Chapter 6 – MECP2

Alex's condition was extremely rare. He was indeed special.

Alex was born with a brain anomaly, an undeveloped Vermis. The diagnosis did not go much beyond that. Not much was known about Alex's situation at the time, and there was a lot of misunderstanding and misinformation. Alex's neurologist, to this day, classifies him as having cerebral palsy[6]. Penny's family thought Alex's brain stem was not attached. It was not until a few years ago, around the time Alex was fourteen or fifteen, that his condition was actually understood.

MECP2[7] is a gene associated with a protein essential to the functioning of nerve cells. The protein likely plays a role in maintaining connections (synapses) between neurons, where cell-to-cell communication occurs. The role of MECP2 in disease is primarily associated with either a loss of function of the MECP2 gene, where necessary proteins are not manufactured as in Rett syndrome, or in a gain of function of the gene (duplication), where proteins are created unnecessarily as in MECP2 duplication syndrome. The structure of the MeCP2 protein or the amount of protein that is produced is critical for communication between neurons.

A large number of mutations in the MECP2 gene have been identified in females with Rett syndrome, a brain disorder that causes problems with communication, learning, and coordination. The condition typically becomes apparent after six to eighteen months of age, predominately in females. Symptoms include problems with language, coordination, and repetitive movements. Often there is slower growth, problems walking, and a smaller head size. Complications can include seizures, scoliosis, and sleeping problems. Those affected, however, may be affected to different degrees.

The MECP2 gene occurs on the X chromosome, and develops as a new mutation, with less than one percent of the cases being inherited from one of the parents. It occurs almost exclusively in girls. There is now genetic testing to confirm the diagnosis based on symptoms.

---

[6] To be fair to Dr. Urion, this is a normal default diagnosis with a condition like Alex's, which was so rare and virtually unknown. Penny and Jerry insist that Dr. Urion gave them hope and helped them believe there was light at the end of the tunnel.

[7] This information was obtained from a quick Google search on the internet. See https://en.wikipedia.org/wiki/MECP2 and https://ghr.nlm.nih.gov/gene/MECP2

Because males have a different chromosome combination than females, boys who have the genetic mutation associated with Rett syndrome (MECP2) are affected in devastating ways (see below). Most die before birth or in early infancy. Alex was already defying the odds at one month of age. He would continue to do so for the rest of his life.

Death is often related to seizure, aspiration pneumonia, malnutrition, and accidents.

None of this was known to Penny and Jerry, or their doctors and the experts they consulted. Actually, still much is not known and the situation is not quite as simple as described above.

An extra copy (duplication) of the MECP2 gene in each cell causes MECP2 duplication syndrome, a condition characterized by intellectual disability, delayed development, and seizures. This condition affects males more often than females. The resulting changes in gene regulation and protein production in the brain lead to abnormal neuronal function. These neuronal changes disrupt normal brain activity, causing the signs and symptoms. When females are affected, they tend to have milder features.

At least nineteen mutations in the MECP2 gene cause MECP2-related severe neonatal encephalopathy. This condition almost exclusively affects males and is characterized by small head size (microcephaly), movement disorders, breathing problems, and seizures. Many of the MECP2 gene mutations that cause this condition in males cause a similar disorder called Rett syndrome in females. How the alteration of the structure of the MeCP2 protein and reduction of the amount of protein that is produced disrupts normal brain development remains unclear.

Other mutations in the MECP2 gene have also been found to cause PPM-X syndrome. This disorder is characterized by mild to severe intellectual disability, bipolar disorder, and a pattern of movement abnormalities known as parkinsonism. This condition affects males more often than females. When females are affected, they tend to have only mild intellectual disability. Issues with regulation of genes in the brain likely plays a role in the development of intellectual disability, and movement and mood disorders in affected individuals.

The MECP2 gene is also associated with autism spectrum and several other disorders, such as moderate to severe X-linked intellectual disability. People with both the features of Rett syndrome and signs and symptoms similar to Angelman syndrome (a condition

25

characterized by intellectual disability, problems with movement, and inappropriate laughter and excitability) also have mutations in the MECP2 gene.

Even the latest information on this disorder is often contradictory and confusing. In the meantime, life went on. Alex learned and grew as any other human child, although a bit differently than most given the challenges confronting him. These challenges he and his parents met with fierce determination and love.

Chapter 7 – Alex, the Early Years

Alex was thirteen months old that October, and just sitting up. On Halloween, Penny's parents went to the shoe store in Charlestown and bought Alex his first pair of shoes. It was a family tradition, just like his birthday parties would become. Whether he would ever walk in them was unknown.

Alex continued to progress through the first part of 1998, although one had to be happy with small gains. To help, Jean, an occupational therapist, began to come out to the apartment to teach him to eat table food.

Penny's Journal (1998):
> **April** – Alex gets up on his hands and knees, and rocks back and forth to learn to crawl.
> **April 13** – Alex rolls from his tummy to his back.
> **April 16** – Alex gets his prone stander. This will help you to get your hips and legs stronger.

By May, Alex was eating his first grilled cheese sandwiches and drinking from a 'sippy' cup, though he still liked his bottle. In mid-May, Alex went to NovaCare to get fitted for a new set of braces. These had hinges on them to give him more movement to help him bend and sit, and learn to take side steps.

Alex knew what 'no' meant. It was a word he heard a lot growing up. He would stop what he was doing when his parents uttered it, but like most kids, went on again, doing what he wanted a short time later.

Alex loved to eat and drink, mostly juice and root beer. He could be very persistent.

Penny – "He'd constantly ask for a drink of juice and pout when he didn't get it."

Alex was working hard with Sandra, his therapist, but always on his own terms. Still, he made the little improvements he had to make. The main objective was to see if he could be taught to walk. Many doubted he ever would, but Penny and Jerry, who saw the determination on his face when he worked with his therapist, knew someday he would. In the meantime, he loved it when Penny blew bubbles at him so he could pop them.

Through the summer, Alex continued to learn and grow. Another therapist, Christine, came to meet Alex and help him to play with toys that had some difficult items to them, like turning the pages of his 'feely bugs' book, and pushing his Pooh walker, which proved difficult. Christine would also build obstacle courses out of the couch cushions, so he could climb over them. As many of his therapist and teachers would do, she used her creativity to engage him and keep him active.

The beginning of July Penny and Jerry took Alex with them to vacation in Maine.

Penny's Journal (1998):
> **July 1**
>> Mommy and Daddy take you on a vacation to Maine with Grammy and Auntie Mary M.
>
> **July 2**
>> You throw your orange ball to Mommy. Daddy takes you over to the grassy park to blow bubbles and to throw the ball.
>
> **July 6**
>> You are now starting to open the drawers in the house – time for locks.

Like any two year old, Alex was starting to engage in the battle of wills. He threw his first and last temper tantrum during his assessment with Christine, when she refused to give him the toy he wanted. Three days later he gave Sandra, his home therapist, a kiss. In early August he went on the Swan Boats in Boston Commons, the first of many such exploits.

Alex had his favorite CDs and toys, like any child. Disney was a big favorite, as was Blue's Clues, about a blue dog. Alex would select a disk from the box and shake it in the air to indicate he wanted to watch it. He knew if you didn't put on the one he asked for. He'd shake the box again in your face.

Alex loved music. One of his favorite games was Learn Thru Music, where you'd hit a key on the toy and the song would change. When Jerry would listen to tapes or a concert on the TV, Alex would lie on the floor and put his ear to the speaker, no matter how loud the music was. Even after Jerry picked him up and moved him away, afraid he'd hurt his ears, Alex would crawl back to the speakers. He couldn't get enough of the musical vibrations.

Alex never seemed to get sick or catch colds, but did have bad allergies, sometimes brought on by a friendly dog or cat. Because of this, Alex didn't have much interaction with animals. Unlike other children, Alex couldn't tell you if he was in pain or not feeling well.

You had to be attuned to him and notice when he wasn't his happy, smiling self.

Jerry – "He would sleep a lot when he didn't feel well. At first when he acted sick, we would rush him to the doctor's, but after awhile, when we found it was never anything serious, we stopped doing that."

Alex was an enigma to the medical profession, his condition not in any of their reference books.

Jerry – "We were out to dinner at the Cape. Alex didn't feel well and passed out. We took him to the nearest hospital in Falmouth, to the emergency room."

Unbeknownst to Penny and Jerry, Alex had a bad case of the flu, but wasn't acting sick. Since he couldn't blow his nose he got stopped up and passed out. It was a frightening experience. He had never passed out like this before. Luckily, it was nothing serious and Alex recovered quickly.

Jerry - "A day or two later we took him back for a check up and the doctor wanted to know if Alex lived in the area, asking if he needed a physician. He seemed very interested in Alex's condition."

Alex was a unique and interesting case.

There were setbacks, like the times he fell at home and broke his foot, then his elbow.

Penny – "He'd fall when he tried to sit down. He'd just plop down hard and land wrong. We'd take him to the hospital and they'd put a cast on him."

They didn't become unduly concerned, and he eventually outgrew this tendency, learning how to sit without hurting himself.

The bones healed and life went on, as did the obstacles.

Any dental work, even a cleaning, was a big issue. Alex couldn't keep his mouth open and would clamp it shut. He had to go to the OR and be sedated to do any work on his teeth, such as a cleaning or a filling. Yet Jerry refused to have all of Alex's teeth removed, which is routine for such cases. Jerry was Alex's advocate. He put himself in Alex's place and realized how losing his teeth would have affected him.

During all this time, he was in Early Intervention, learning new skills, although very slowly. One of the first things he was taught, and one of the most important for his well-being, was how to get into and out of the van, for that would be his chariot to the world, and Alex would go everywhere.

Penny and Jerry experienced the joy of parenthood, with all the optimism and happiness loving parents can have.

Penny's Journal: (1998)

Sept 25 - Today you go to your first little boy's hair cut. Mommy and Daddy and Grammy took you to Vincent's Clip Joint in Lynn and you sat on a carousel horsey. Now you look just like a little boy, no more baby look, but you're still Mommy's baby.

Sept 26 - "Now you are Two" Today is your 2nd birthday and we're having a party with a choo-choo train cake. All your relatives and friends are here to celebrate with you. You had such a good day, having fun and playing with your friends.

Alex continued to make progress with his therapy.

Sept 28 - Today you saw Dr. Urion at Children's Hospital. He was so happy to see you crawling and babbling. Today you even said hi to Da Da and Mommy.

Penny and Jerry put Alex in the van and took him to the Aquarium to see the penguins, the fishes, and the sea lion, which he liked very much. That Halloween Alex dressed up as a little devil and went trick-or-treating to their parents' and relatives' houses (Nana and Papa, Uncle Joey and Auntie Kim with cousin Emma, Uncle Jim and Auntie Mary, and Grammy).

Alex was using his 'sippy' cup more, only getting one bottle a day just before bed time. He was eating using a spoon by himself. Penny took him to the Magenta Group (sensory skills), where he did well. Penny writes in her journal that Alex seemed to like this group, so different from the 'Mommy and Me Group' (just Penny and Alex). He did Snack Time, and Circle Time, and even drew a picture of a sea creature.

He was standing longer and straighter, and beginning to take side steps and 'creeping' steps. He was growing normally. He was learning more each day.

Penny's Journal:

Nov 11 - Alex, you are getting to be Mommy and Daddy's big boy. You are learning to do so much everyday and we are very proud of you and love you so much. You will do things at your own time.

30

In early January of the new year, 1999, Alex started the Blue Group, where they focused on sensory drills, and began making new friends. Making friends was something Alex was good at. He would have many friends in the end.

On January 11, his therapist, Sandra, brought in a walker, his first, and Alex walked around the parlor rug with her help. A few days later he had another MRI.

All focus was on trying to teach Alex to walk. The hope was that he would walk by five, otherwise, they were told he would never walk. So every small success was celebrated.

Penny's Journal (1999)-

Jan 24 -Today you took 4 steps while Grammy was holding your hands. And with Sandra's help, you took 15 steps toward the television and 10 steps to Daddy and Mommy.

Jan 28 - Today you saw Dr. Urion. He was so happy to see you pulling up and holding Daddy's hands and taking steps. Your MRI showed your Myelin[8] was getting closer to normal. That's good news...baby.

By early February Alex is no longer using a bottle.

Feb 20 - Today Mommy and Daddy took you for your second haircut. You didn't like it, but you look like a little boy, so cute you are.

April 4 - Today Mommy and Daddy took you to Children's Hospital for an EKG, and Dr. Urion told us that there are no seizures. He said if you're not paying attention, it's just behavioral. Also today we gave your prone stander to Tri City Center. This way, children who can use it now can.

April 31 - Today you can get your new braces. These braces just go inside your sneakers. These braces will help you with balance and get you to walk.

May 6 -Today you got a new walker. This one is a lot heavier for you to use.

May 11 -Today at school you walked from the bathroom to the motor[9] room with Danielle. That's about 20 – 25 steps.

---

[8] Myelin – is a sheath or fatty-coating around our nerves. Alex's low myelination had resolved itself.
[9] Motor Skills Room

In early April, a coordinator working with Dr. Urion, noted that Alex was avoiding eye contact with her, looking blank, and not responding. "Something's wrong," she told his parents and the doctor. They brought him in for some tests and determined that everything was all right. He wasn't having seizures. He just didn't like the coordinator's style. She would get in his face and talk loudly to him. He was shy with strangers and didn't respond well to that kind of treatment. They got a different coordinator to work with Alex.

Early in June the family jumped in the van and vacationed at the Cape with Jerry's mother. They went to Falmouth and stayed at a place with the beach right out their back door. Alex enjoyed himself playing in the sand and watching the boats, even getting onto the ledge from the sand by himself.

Figure 2- Alex at the beach

But as sometimes would happen, he got sick after going to the beach -

(1999)
June – Today was a sad day. Mommy and daddy had to take you to Children's Hospital because you weren't feeling good. The doctors at

the Children's Hospital wanted you to stay overnight so you could get better. Mommy and Daddy were with you all the time. The next day you came home feeling a lot better.

Alex recovered quickly. That Fourth of July they went to Penny's brother, Jim's camp for a picnic and had a blast. Alex had his crawling knee-pads on and crawled all over the trailer site. He held hands and walked with his mother and aunt, and had a hamburger and a hot-dog. The best part was he went splashing in the lake. He loved the water and was now bathing in the tub.

> **July 13** -Today you started pool (water) therapy with Mary Ellen. Mommy's so proud of you, your first time and you did so good.
> **July 20 – 22** - Today you had to go to Children's Hospital to stay for a few days.

During another vacation to Cape Cod with Jerry's mom, they went to the beach again, where Alex seemed mesmerized by the big waves. Penny thought he'd be afraid, but he seemed to like it a lot.

As Alex approached his third birthday, around the end of August, Early Intervention came to an end. Penny and Alex said good-bye to Sandra, Colleen, and Ann, and to the Toddler Group in the city. A new phase in Alex's life was about to begin. A visit to Dr. Millis, his Orthopedic physician, ended with Alex not wearing his SMOs (braces) for three months on a trial basis.

In the beginning of September, Alex started at the Shore Collaborative, a state-funded preschool for ages two and a half to five, where he would have physical, occupational, and speech therapy, and learn to communicate. He would attend this program for the next two years.

> **Sept 9** -Today was your first day of school at Shore Collaborative. Daddy and Mommy took you to school to meet your teacher, Pam, and two aides, Karen and Mary. You also got to meet Katarina and David, your classmates, also Sarah. You had a terrific first day. You painted an apple and the teachers put it on the door with the apple tree.
> **Sept 26** -Today you are three years old. Mommy and Daddy had a big birthday party and all your relatives and friends came to celebrate with you. Your birthday cake was your favorite characters, Blue's Clues, Arthur, Barney, Pooh, Tigger, Elmo, La La Teletubby, and Dalmatian Puppy. Mommy and Daddy got you lots of balloons also. You had a

great day. You were so tired you fell asleep on the floor. HAPPY
BIRTHDAY ALEX!

Later, in October, Alex went on a school field trip to a farm,
where he petted the goats and rode a pony, which like most children,
he liked. He next attended his Uncle Joey and Aunt Kim's wedding,
where his father carried him up the aisle in his tuxedo. Penny wrote in
the journal how handsome he looked.

They lived in Everett at the time, in a second story apartment,
reached by a long flight of steep stairs. Either Penny or Jerry would
carry Alex up and down all day, every day, without complaint. They
were intent on making sure Alex would have a happy, full, normal life.
They took him with them everywhere they went, making Alex the
center of their active and vibrant lives.

> **Dec 12 -** Mommy and Daddy took you to see Santa Claus. You gave
> him big smiles when Mommy sat you on his lap.
> **Dec 22 -** Santa came to visit you and all your friends in school today.
> You got a musical book.
> **Dec 31 -** Mommy and Daddy took you on your first train ride in
> Boston to see the ice sculptures and parade for New Years.

Penny stopped writing in her journal soon after that. Life was getting
too hectic and demanding to write about it in a book any more.

Chapter 8 – The Move to Malden (Forestdale)

The Gentiles moved to Malden when Alex turned five years old. It was a critical time, not only for Alex, but for the city as well. Malden was undergoing some important changes and many Special Needs programs and activities were just coming into existence. These would have a profound impact on Alex's life, but so, too, Alex would have a strong effect on these programs.

One of the most important of these was the Pace Program, where Special Needs students were made part of the regular student body in the city schools. The city elementary and high schools had two or three Special Needs classrooms, where these children received special training, but at all other times, in the cafeteria, the hallways, and the gym, they mingled with the other kids.

Alex had the good fortune to attend the Forestdale School from grade one through the eighth grade. It was an exceptional program. He was able to go to school with the same kids and teachers for the whole time, some of whom, special needs and typical, would become his lifelong friends.

There was a real, meaningful interaction between the Special Needs kids and the regular student body. For instance, students could trade-off their recess or lunch period to go to the Special Needs classrooms and play with the kids or help the teacher. At first, this was just an informal way to get the kids together, but it became a part of the optional curriculum, where students could go and work with the Special Needs class to earn credits. This not only led to lifelong friendships between Alex and some of these extraordinary children, but some were inspired by it to go on and get degrees in Special Education. They are now working with and helping others (see Chapter 21). However, it took some learning to get it right.

When Penny's friend, Mary Gasdia's oldest girl, Carianna, was in pre-school they had special needs kids in the same class as the typical kids, who acted as examples, but there was a little autistic boy who the paras couldn't handle, and he targeted Mary's daughter.

"No one told us about this or explained the policy. We were completely unaware of what was going on. My daughter became distraught when I dropped her off at school in the morning. She started out OK, but after the third or forth day she no longer wanted to go to school."

Mary went in with her and sat in the class room to see what the matter was.

Mary - "It was terrible. This boy attacked her and pushed her down."

Although her daughter did not suffer any serious harm, she could have. They left that school as a result of the incident. The school learned an important lesson that helped move inclusion forward.

Alex's first teacher at Forestdale was Dawn Frim, who taught him from five years old to eight. She remembers him well.

"I worked with Alex from 2002 to 2004. I started teaching in 2000 at the Beebe School, where Alex was first going to go. We went down to check out the Special Needs room and saw that it was small and cramped, and full of equipment, with no space for the children. Jerry threatened to go across the street to the fire department and report them as a fire hazard the first day Alex went to school there."

The class was moved to Forestdale.

Jerry and Penny were the only parents who went and saw what was happening.

Dawn has two masters' degrees in Special Ed and has been teaching for thirty-two years. Recently retired, she still keeps in touch with some of her students, who are now in their twenties. She has worked with a wide mix of Special Needs children and tried to make it a habit during her career to change her focus every five or so years to stay up on things.

Dawn - "When I started working with kids like Alex and his friend, James, with such severe disabilities, I went back to school to take classes in how to handle things like seizures, and to learn more about the different disabilities, how to feed kids through tubes, how to teach language to kids with gross motor skill needs. My specialty was autism, but I had kids with cerebral palsy, and non-specific special needs and development issues, like Alex."

Each class had a teacher, three paras, who acted as assistants, and a nurse.

Dawn - "I tried to keep the kids as mobile as possible, to keep them moving and improving their motor skills."

Often the kids had additional health problems and risks.

"One boy would turn blue after any physical exertion. He died young. Alex wasn't like that. He was sturdy and strong."

Dawn expected him to beat the odds. She did not expect him to die young.

Dawn - "You have to have patience as a Special Ed teacher, and be happy with small victories."

When Alex hadn't learned to walk by five years old, many thought he would never walk. Some gave up on him, but Penny and Jerry never did. Penny didn't worry. She knew he would walk when he was ready, in his own time. Some suggested that they should discontinue or cut back on the therapies designed to teach Alex to walk.

When Jerry heard this he slammed his hand on the table and objected. It didn't happen.

Dawn – "Jerry could be demanding when it came to his kid."

Jerry – "Because of budget cuts, in the IEP meetings, they were always trying to take stuff away. It got worse as Alex grew older, but we said no."

Jerry stood up to the administrators and let them know the parents were the boss.

Jerry – "We were Alex's voice."

Alex was going to have every opportunity to grow and develop, even if it didn't meet the experts' timetables.

Then a miracle occurred.

Dawn – "One day at Forestdale, Alex, who was eight and half at the time, took his first steps unaided, without his walker, on his own. We threw a party. It was a big deal."

Up to then, he had only crawled around on his knees to move about. They would balance him by his hands like a twelve-month-old. This was a major development. Alex had done something many said he would never do. They celebrated this small event as if it was an Olympic medal.

"It was unbelievable," continued Dawn. "Everyone yelled and clapped. Everyone was laughing and Alex had a great big smile on his face. It was a very memorable day."

When Penny walked into the school to get him, Alex walked out to greet her. She couldn't believe her eyes, and broke down in tears. She knew he would walk someday, in his own time. It wasn't so much optimism as belief in her child.

Dawn made Alex laugh a lot.

"You have to be creative to engage these kids, even to the point of antics. We did a lot of different things to occupy them."

Dawn developed a computer game with buttons of different colors and picture icons.

"Alex used to like it," Dawn said. "He would love to press the blue button and go to the ocean and the beach, and go on the boat to catch the sharks. I used pictures of the kids' faces to make the game fun. Each face caused a different song and scene to come up. It's an adaptive technique using software programs (IntelliKeys) that I learned from school and adapted for my class."

Penny – "Alex didn't have good motor skills. He couldn't push or hit a button, and even when he did, his hand would slide off."

Dawn's simple exercise helped to improve these skills.

Alex also liked the Shel Silverstein books of poems and pictures (a language lesson), like 'A Light in the Attic' book. The kids would hold the pictures while she said the poem. Alex liked the 'Dirty Old Man' pictures and poem the best (from 'Where the Sidewalk Ends').

Dawn - "He always chose this picture and poem, and would laugh when it was read. It made it enjoyable."

The poem starts as follows:

Oh' I'm Dirty Dan, the
World's dirtiest man, I never
Have taken a shower.
I can't see my shirt, it's so
Covered with dirt, and my
Ears have enough to grow
Flowers...

The part that made Alex laugh is:

I live in a pen, with
Three hogs and a hen...

Sometimes they would act out the poem.

Dawn - "We were very animated. The kids would laugh. It was fun."

One of the kids, Alex's best friend, James, said his first word, "dirty," while playing the game.

"It was very creative," continued Dawn. "We used many modalities, sign language, gestures, expressions, music, anything to stimulate them and get them involved."

Alex was able to associate pictures with certain words at this time, like his Mommy and Daddy, a skill he seemed to have lost in later years, according to Dawn.

"The kids were in tune and knew what was going to happen, like when it was nap time or story time."

Dawn was amazed by how much Penny and Jerry cared, how they participated in everything.

"Penny and Jerry got to me," Dawn told me.

At one point, in 2004, the school decided to take Dawn out of that class. She had a lot of experience with autistic kids and the school wanted her to teach a class with those children. She wanted to stay with the class she had, and Penny and Jerry wanted her to stay with Alex, as well, but she had no say in the matter. In the end, even with the parents behind her, she had to leave.

While she was with Alex, Dawn had open classes and invited the parents to join them, the more the better.

Dawn – "Many teachers don't care for this, but I liked it when the parents took part and took an interest in the children."

She felt it could only help.

"I believed this so strongly that even if the parent was a real 'a-hole' that no one liked, I would still invite them to come."

A few did, but it was very rare. Penny was there almost every day for part of the class.

Figure 3- Alex graduates the eighth grade

Dawn's first impression of Penny and Jerry was that they were loving parents and heavily invested in their child's welfare. She found this unusual.

Dawn - "A lot of parents aren't that involved. They would drop off their kids and return to pick them up. Not Penny. We were lucky when one parent would show up at Parents' Night. Penny was there every time! She was a parent role model. You could depend on her. She was a go-to person. Maybe you'd find five out of a thousand parents like Penny and Jerry."

As would be the case with most of those who were close to Alex and helped him, Dawn found that Alex helped her in return.

"I was having a lot of personal problems at the time, going through a divorce, taking care of my mother, who was in her eighties. I was under a lot of stress, but when I looked at how Penny and Jerry were dealing with their challenges, it gave me the inspiration and strength to get through things. They were such loving parents with such a positive life attitude. Everything was centered around Alex."

Dawn was impressed by how they fought for Alex's rights, like when Jerry objected to his first classroom.

When I asked Dawn what kind of temperament and skills you need to teach Special Ed, she told me creativity was the most important thing, next to understanding.

"You must be patient and be happy with small gains, like getting a smile."

After working with severe Special Needs students for the day she would often go home exhausted.

"Sometimes it takes so much work to get so little back."

Dawn's approach was unique, but was adapted by some of the para-professionals she worked with. She has worked with severely violent autistic children, who have become successful and are now working, with a good job and family.

In spite of the difficulties, she gets a lot of satisfaction helping parents and changing the students' lives for the better.

"It's a very rewarding feeling," Dawn insists.

Alex was lucky. Not only did his parents participate and fight for his rights and well-being, there were special programs at Malden, where they now lived, to meet Alex's needs. It wasn't always like that, and even now, it's not like that everywhere.

Chapter 9 – The Old Way

In the 1950's, until the Civil Rights movements in the 1960s, a Special Needs child, a handicapped child, as they were known, with severe disabilities like Alex had, could expect a life of loneliness and neglect. Unfortunately, that can still be the case in some places, even now in the twenty-first century.

Before the enactment of laws written to protect Special Needs individuals, these children were routinely put away in institutions 'for their own good and the good of society', an expert recently explained (see below). Many disabled people living in hospitals, special segregated schools, and care homes, were known to have suffered severe emotional and physical abuse.

Of course, there were many good and dedicated doctors and nurses at these facilities, but a child with special needs left alone in an institution or home like this was at the mercy of the weakest link in the system. Some of them showed little respect for their charges.

Victoria Brignell[10] reports that, "Staff often made little attempt to empathize with disabled people's experiences, denying them autonomy, choice, and dignity, and at times deliberately caused them pain and discomfort. In care homes and special schools for disabled children, there was sometimes hardly any attempt to meet the children's emotional needs or acknowledge their individual identities."

Even in the 1960s, an impersonal regime, where the children's possessions are numbered and staff does not play or talk effectively with them, was still the norm. Often, there was little real emotional support for Special Needs kids, let alone inclusion. They were left alone, neglected, and shunned.

For example, not only did the institution that was being reported have substandard toilets, but children in the upstairs wards had no access to the grounds.

Victoria Brignell again - "Little attempt was made to give the children any mental stimulation. Televisions were provided, but for the benefit of the staff rather than the children. None of the staff took the trouble to try to communicate with those children who had speech impairments. Many of the children communicated with each other for

[10] Victoria Brignell reports for the BBC. This series is available on the New Statesmen web site on the Internet

years while the staff assumed they were making unintelligible, meaningless noises. If a child cried, the policy was to punish him or her. This punishment consisted of locking the crying child in a small, dark storeroom."

In her series, Victoria gives only a few examples of the ways in which disabled people in institutions have been abused and neglected, right up to recent times. Even though many of the examples she cites are from Great Britain, she maintains the same was and is true in the United States. She insists that these examples are just the tip of a very large iceberg.

Without a diligent, determined, involved, and loving parent to watch over, protect, and fight for them, an institutionalized child is at the mercy of the system, a system that can be cruel as well as uncaring. The real scale of the suffering may never be known.

Alex's life is an example of how things can be different.

In 1972, legislation was introduced in Congress after several landmark court cases, establishing in law the right to education for all handicapped children. On November 19, 1975, Congress enacted Public Law 94-142, also known as, The Education for All Handicapped Children Act of 1975. Things changed, but slowly. As late as 1977, right here in Waltham, MA, institutionalized handicapped patients were routinely buried without a service when they died. In a hole marked only by a letter indicating their religion, and a number indicating their order of burial, they ended their lives of loneliness and neglect in a nameless grave.

Unfortunately, even with laws for their protection, without a local network of support services, bringing up and caring for a disabled child is still a daunting challenge. In some places, it may still be just as bad as it was fifty years ago, with small, cramped, over-crowded, and unhealthy classrooms segregated from the surrounding society (like Alex faced when first starting school), and Special Needs children and adults left to the mercy of happenstance.

Some experts say that the mentally disabled impart an important lesson for our society.

The role of friendship in caring for a mentally disabled person means you have to get closer to them. You do this by helping them with tasks that their disability makes it harder for them to do, like eating, dressing, or moving about. In doing this you learn about yourself and that person, you grow.

You can't do this if the Special Needs are segregated away.

As we will see in the coming pages of this book, those who work with and become friends with people with special needs get as much back as they give. It enriches their lives.

Even in the 1950s there were parents who directly confronted negative attitudes toward disability and challenged a society that tried to isolate and ignore them. The reasons given for hiding them away were many - shame, guilt, belief that they couldn't be taught or were less than human, even for their own good!

These parents, who refused to accept such reasoning, successfully raised money for their cause, enabling associations to continue their fight. This was the first time that parents had taken such direct action to highlight their cause. They were not prepared to wait, they wanted change immediately.

Jerry and Penny were fighting this battle in the 1990s. They are still fighting it.

Chapter 10 – Other Special Needs

So far we have focused on Alex's special needs, but as you can gather from Dawn Frim's comments above, the school where Alex was going included children with a variety of needs, including autism and cerebral palsy, to mention a few. We will be coming across additional conditions requiring special care and training as in Alex's case. For this reason, it might be a good idea to stop and talk a bit about other, so-called disabilities, so we can distinguish them from Alex's and see how they all require the same basic thing - understanding and acceptance.

Autism

Autism[11], or autism spectrum disorder (ASD), refers to a broad range of conditions characterized by challenges with social skills, repetitive behaviors, speech, and nonverbal communication. There appear to be many types of autism. It is highly variable, with several levels of severity, and each person with autism can have unique challenges. Autism is often accompanied by medical issues, such as gastrointestinal (GI) disorders, seizures, and sleep disturbances.

A combination of genetic and environmental factors influence the development of the condition. Autism is fairly common, affecting an estimated one in fifty-nine children, and seems to be increasing slowly over time. Many people with autism also have sensory issues, which can include aversions to certain sights, sounds, and other sensations.

Parents usually notice signs of autism during the first two or three years of their child's life[12]. These signs often develop gradually, though some children with autism reach their developmental milestones at a normal pace before worsening.

Although autism has a strong genetic basis, there are many risk factors associated with it, including certain infections during pregnancy, such as rubella, as well as exposure to toxins such as alcohol, cocaine, pesticides, and severe pollution while pregnant. There is some controversy surrounding other supposed risk facts, such as vaccines. The immune system is also thought to play an important role in autism.

Autism affects information processing in the brain by altering how nerve cells and their synapses connect and organize. How this occurs is

---

[11] From https://www.autismspeaks.org/what-autism

[12] See https://en.wikipedia.org/wiki/Autism)

not well understood. Although there is no known cure there have been cases of children who recovered. However, not many children with autism live independently after reaching adulthood, though as Dawn mentions, some are successful, having jobs and families.

Autism is estimated to affect 24.8 million people globally, as of 2015. In 2017, about 1.5% of the children in western countries were diagnosed with ASD, more than doubling in the United States from 0.7% in 2000. It occurs four-to-five times more often in boys than girls. The number of people diagnosed has increased dramatically since the 1960s, partly due to changes in diagnostic practice. The question of whether actual rates have increased is unresolved.

Many autistic children appear normal, and can run and play just like any other kid. It is only when you interact with an autistic child that you can see the difficult challenges they and their parents must face. For more on this condition and its symptoms and screening, see https://en.wikipedia.org/wiki/Autism.

Down Syndrome

Down syndrome[13] is a generic disorder caused by an extra chromosome (chromosome 21). Down syndrome is typically associated with growth delays and small stature, poor to moderate intellectual ability, and characteristic facial features, such as upward slanting eyes. The average young adult with Down syndrome has the mental ability of an eight or nine-year-old child, but this can vary widely.

The extra chromosome is believed to occur by chance, with no known behavioral or environmental risk factors, although its frequency increases with the age of the mother. Down syndrome can be identified during pregnancy, and many are terminated. Some say Down syndrome may soon disappear because of this. However, as with all children with special needs, education and proper care have been shown to improve quality of life for both parent and child.

Down syndrome is one of the most common genetic abnormalities in humans in the United States. It occurs in about one per 1,000 babies born each year. In 2015, Down syndrome was present in 5.4 million individuals. It is named after John Langdon Down, a British doctor who fully described the syndrome in 1866. Abortion

---

[13] From https://en.wikipedia.org/wiki/Down_syndrome

rates range from 61% to 93% in the US depending on the population group.

About 20% of adults with Down syndrome in the US have paying jobs in some capacity, though many require a sheltered work environment. Most adults with this condition continue to need considerable support to be independent. Life expectancy for a person with Down syndrome is around 50 to 60 years with proper health care.

Those with Down syndrome nearly always have physical and intellectual disabilities. They may also typically have poor immune functions and an increased risk of a number of other health problems, including congenital heart defects, epilepsy, leukemia, thyroid disease, and mental disorders. Children and adults with Down syndrome are also at increased risk of epileptic seizures, but typically do fairly well with social skills. Behavior problems are not generally as great an issue as in other syndromes associated with intellectual disability. For more detail on symptoms, risks, causes, and screening see https://en.wikipedia.org/wiki/Down_syndrome.

Cerebral Palsy

Cerebral palsy[14] is a group of neurological disorders caused by a brain injury or abnormality that happens before, during, or immediately after birth, while the brain is still developing. It is the most common cause of physical disability occurring in childhood, taking place approximately in 1 in 323 children. An estimated 764,000 people live with cerebral palsy in the United States.

Cerebral palsy can also be caused by a poor oxygen supply to the brain during birth, as well as infections or exposure to some toxins or chemicals during pregnancy. In addition, premature infants are at a higher risk for cerebral palsy. Severe illness during the first years of life, physical injury, and severe dehydration can also lead to cerebral palsy

The disorder affects a person's ability to control their motor functions or movement. Between one-third and one-half of children with cerebral palsy also have a seizure disorder and some degree of intellectual disability, according to WebMD. The main effects of cerebral palsy are poor muscle coordination, motor skills, and overall body movement. People with cerebral palsy have difficulty controlling certain body movements or cannot control them at all. The condition can also affect a person's posture and balance, depending on the

---

[14] See https://www.everydayhealth.com/cerebral-palsy/

individual, although more than half of people with cerebral palsy can walk on their own.

Cerebral palsy is a permanent condition, but many therapies and treatments can help people manage their condition and improve their quality of life. It is not a progressive disorder, meaning that the underlying brain damage does not worsen with time.

A variety of other conditions often occur in people who have cerebral palsy. For example, about forty-one percent of children with cerebral palsy have epilepsy and about seven percent have an autism spectrum condition. Other common co-occurring conditions include learning disabilities, chronic pain, ADHD, mental health conditions, and vision, hearing, or speech problems. Cerebral palsy can also lead to several complications resulting from the muscle and coordination difficulties it causes.

As with Alex, most people with cerebral palsy will need an interdisciplinary team of healthcare providers, including a pediatrician, neurologist, mental health practitioner, orthopedic surgeon, physical therapist, speech therapist, occupational therapist, and others.

Most children with cerebral palsy live into adulthood, and many of those adults work, have families, and are active in their communities. The life expectancy of people with cerebral palsy is different for each person. Those with more severe cases usually have a shorter life expectancy than the average person or those with mild or moderate cerebral palsy. Other factors, such as early aging, a weakened immune system, overall disabilities, and musculoskeletal disorders can also affect how long a person with cerebral palsy lives. For more on cerebral palsy see https://www.everydayhealth.com/cerebral-palsy/.

Other Special Needs

There are many other, what can we call them? Handicaps is the word that most often comes to mind, and was used for many years to designate those with special needs like Alex, but that word just doesn't cut it anymore. To call someone handicapped is to define them by their disabilities, and as we will see with Alex, that's just not possible. Nor is it very helpful or edifying. Knowing and working with people like Alex is enriching in many ways, as well as educational. It teaches us about ourselves. These people are not special because of their handicaps, however these are perceived, but in spite of them.

Other special needs[15] might include such things as muscular dystrophy, multiple sclerosis, chronic asthma, and epilepsy. Things like dyslexia and other processing disorders, or emotional/behavioral issues like bi-polar disorder and oppositional defiance disorder, are special needs, as is sensory impairment like blindness and deafness.

An individual with special needs may need help with communication, movement, self care and decision-making[16] In addition to those mentioned above, other special needs include ADHD (Attention Deficit Hyper-Activity), uncontrolled anger, reading and learning disabilities, intellectual disabilities, pervasive developmental disorder, spina bifida, traumatic brain injury, and cystic fibrosis. Special needs can also include such conditions as cleft lips and/or palates, port-wine stains, and missing limbs.

Many children - like Alex until he was fourteen years old - have no diagnosis and are often arbitrarily denoted as having a non-specific or developmental issue, or, as in Alex's case, labeled as cerebral palsy for lack of a better name.

The types of special needs vary in severity, and even within the same classification like autism or Down syndrome, can range significantly. For educational purposes, a student with special needs is classified as being a severe case when their IQ is between twenty and thirty-five.

Obviously, different needs require different training and treatments, as well as services focused on their specific requirements. No two Special Needs children are the same, yet each is no different than you or me, and all of them, with the proper love and attention, can have full, happy, and meaningful lives.

---

[15] See https://pbwslaw.com/special_needs_children_rights/

[16] Also see https://study.com/academy/lesson/what-is-special-needs-definition-types-law.html and
https://en.wikipedia.org/wiki/Special_needs

Chapter 11 – The Sitters

Penny had a lot of help. We've already seen how Jerry's mother provided critical support in the first years. They also had a professional Day Care sitter, Ryan, who came in twice a week. In addition to this, Penny had her own network of friends, family, and neighbors, who would pitch in and give her a hand so that Penny and Jerry could go out once in awhile.

One of Penny's best friends is Cindy Kelloway, who worked at the Malden Trust Bank with her and Jerry. Other than family, Cindy and Paul, her husband, are two of Jerry's oldest friends, and were there at the beginning.

"Bobbi Jo MacDonald was a good friend of Penny's," Cindy told me. "Her three daughters, Skye, Aryzona, and Shawna were good friends with Alex, and used to go with their mom when she babysat for him. They were very close. I remember another close friend of Penny's, Emily, who babysat for Alex during 2008 and lived with them for awhile."

Cindy, too, would pitch in and watch Alex.

"I would babysit often when they went to concerts and things. I used to change him and feed him and put him to bed, dress him, things like that. His parents would try to take care of all of these things, but sometimes I had to do it. After they left to go out, Alex would sit by the door and reach up for it, pouting and whining for about twenty minutes, then he'd be fine. He missed them. We used to watch TV and cuddle on the couch until he fell asleep. I stopped after Alex turned twelve. I felt uncomfortable taking care of him as he grew older."

Cindy, who went to all the birthday parties, and took movies at many of them, would move him around to make sure everyone paid attention to him. Alex knew when it was party time.

Cindy – "Alex had bad allergies that would make him cough. He would fill up with mucus, but he couldn't blow his nose to clear it. It caused trouble breathing. He had to take Zyrtec."

Cindy also talked about Jerry's mother.

"She was a wonderful person, and used to take care of Alex all the time. Everyone wanted to be with her and meet her. She had black-gray hair and dark skin. There's a nice picture of her and Alex. She took Penny in and became her second mother. I just loved her."

Cindy is not the only one to feel this way.

Alex was never potty-trained, although they tried to teach him at school, but Penny and Jerry didn't follow through. They thought using diapers was safer. Ryan, their professional para, agreed.

Ryan - "Alex's condition did not allow potty training. He had to have slip-on diapers. It was really not a problem."

Marlene, Penny's sister, would also babysit occasionally.

"I used to babysit with Alex when he was younger, once when Penny and Jerry went to Foxwoods for the weekend. Alex was a wonderful child and easy to take care of. We played 'Ring around the rosy'. It made him laugh."

Another person who used to help out was Penny's next door neighbor, Paula English.

"I moved into the house across the street in 2000. Before I got to know them, I would sit on the steps and watch them. Then as Alex got older, I saw how the father would whisk him up and put him in the car to take him somewhere. I came to admire them for how they took care of their boy."

Paula and Penny really connected around four years ago when they started scrapbooking together.

Paula - "She just has so much energy and is so talented, I really admire her, always have, just adored them. I've never seen a child who had that much love, even for children without special needs. It's always astonished me in a good way. They are just incredible parents. It was amazing how they cared for him."

She would visit Penny often, and slowly got to know Alex.

"That smile just got me. I did a photo shoot for them in the park and tried to get him to smile. It wasn't easy, but after that he would always smile when he saw me."

Then one day Penny called and asked her to sit with Alex.

"I said, wow, I was honored, but a little worried, afraid at first something might happen, but it was no problem. It went on from there."

Penny – "Alex knew when he did something bad, and we had to punish him."

Alex would take the cable-box off the top of the cabinet and throw it behind the TV. Penny and Jerry never lost their temper. Penny would explain to him.

"Now you broke the TV, you can't watch your programs."

He somehow knew he was being punished, and would sit there and pout.

Then one day they came home after a night out and found that Alex hadn't slept all night. Their not being there broke his routine, a routine he countered on. He was six years old. Penny and Jerry never left Alex alone overnight again

Ryan LaRoche was a professional Special Needs para at the Malden elementary school system where Alex was going. Later on he was their professional Day Care sitter, who came in twice a week, Tuesdays and Wednesdays, from 2:30 to 6:00 pm.

"He was my right hand man," said Penny. "You could count on Ryan. He was really dependable and trustworthy. He was good with Alex. Alex really responded to him."

Jerry and Penny loved him. So did Alex.

Ryan is from Wakefield and went to Wakefield High School, where he graduated in 1998. He has known Alex for fourteen years, since 2004, when Alex was about eight and going to Forestdale where Ryan was a para. He had been there for three years when he met Alex.

"We had four kids in the class when Alex arrived. James, his friend was there. I assisted Bethany, the Special Ed teacher, and worked with the students. I'd go outside with them, and to the gym and art class, where they worked with clay and drawing with markers and crayons."

According to Ryan, Alex stood out.

"He was always laughing and smiling, at least, most of the time. He was a happy kid, always wanting to be tickled."

Ryan left teaching after three years, in 2007, and is now a reporter and editor for the Daily Times Chronicle in Woburn. He continued to see Alex two days a week, sitting four hours on Tuesdays and Wednesdays.

His first impression of Penny and Jerry was that they were very hands-on parents, who wanted to know what was going on.

"They were aggressive in a good way, not trying to tell you what to do, but engaged in the well-being of their child."

The babysitting service was provided through a government program, the PCA or Personal Care Attendant Program, where working parents could hire people to care for their Special Needs children during the day. It was paid for by the State of Massachusetts.

Ryan had to feed him, as well as change his diapers. Alex would let you know what he wanted.

"Alex would reach in and grab the video he wanted to see."

And when he didn't feel well?

"You could tell by the look on his face if he was feeling all right. If he wasn't smiling he was sick. If he was mad he would frown."

Alex didn't do what he didn't want to do.

"I said no a lot," Ryan said laughing.

Alex was affectionate.

"If you put your face close to his, he would kiss you."

At first, in the beginning, Alex was just one of Ryan's students. He had a professional, objective attitude that he had with most of the kids, with little personal relationship. As time went on, however, as he babysat for him, it got to be more personal.

Ryan - "I really enjoyed spending time with him. I get a feeling of satisfaction from helping people, helping Penny and Jerry so they could work; helping Alex do things on his own, like eat and drink."

Ryan said Alex could stab food on his fork and get it into his mouth on his own. These little victories, however trivial sounding, were huge advances for Alex and helped his parents. Alex was using his walker by this time, when he was fourteen years old, but he could walk on his own if he wanted. Jerry installed a railing in the hallway to assist him.

Ryan stopped baby-sitting for Alex in 2016, but he still took part in his life, going to the yearly birthday parties.

Ryan - "I was part of Team Alex at the Special Olympics. We wore T-shirts with Alex's name on them. After the games, we would all go to Papa Gino's for pizza and sit together at the tables. Alex liked pizza."

When I asked Ryan what it took to be a para for Special Needs children, he said it takes patience.

Ryan - "Patience is the key. You've got to be adaptable and creative. If something doesn't work, you have to try something else. Sometimes you have to give them space and try again later. You have to do the same things every day and repeat things over and over again, though it was never a battle of wills with Alex. It can be difficult at times. It's not the easiest job in the world, but very rewarding when you finally see progress, however small."

Even though Alex was non-verbal, Ryan said Alex knew what was going on around him and was engaged. He was independent and wouldn't let anyone push him around. If he didn't want to do something, he didn't do it.

"Taking care of Alex was more fun than anything," Ryan told me. I'm sure all Alex's babysitters would agree.

Chapter 12 – Special Olympics

The Malden Day Games became part of the Special Olympics in the early 2000s, just at the time Alex and his parents arrived in the city. It was started by Dana Brown, director of the community's school program, and Barbara Scibelli, who was the guiding force behind it.

Dana Brown – "The idea was to invite all the Malden public schools to the stadium at the end of the school year, in May, and have our own Special Olympics. It just happened that Alex was starting at the Forestdale middle school at that time. That's when Team Alex was born. That was the kick-start of what we would later do at the high school."

Team Alex was made up of family and friends, about twenty people in all, who would go to the event.

Penny – "We had T-shirts, a different color each year. One year we had 'I'm Alex' stenciled on it. Another time it said 'Go Alex' on the front and 'Team Alex' on the back. We wore white the first year."

Through the school, Alex trained and participated every year in May, from age eight to twenty-one. The kids would take the day off from school to participate and watch. Alex would take part in the 25 meter and 50 meter assisted walk, and the softball throw.

Figure 4- Team Alex, including left to right, Paul and Cindy, Jerry, Alex, Marlene, Mary Ann, Sheila (behind), Penny, Nicky (behind), Jen-Jen, Kay, Alyssa, Shawna, Annabelle (behind), Sam, Aryzona, Skye, Booby Jo, Sam

John and Sheila Krupcheck were part of Team Alex with their three children, Annabelle, Nicholas, and Genevieve.

"We went each summer," John told me, "once a year in May. All the kids would go and cheer in their T-shirts. Sheila and Penny would go to AC Moore and buy the shirts, about twenty, all the same color, a different color each year."

Penny would negotiate with the store manager for so many of each size. Then she would go home to Sheila's house (she had all the material) and print out the text and iron it on the T-shirts, front and back. Sheila told me that they were always able to get their kids out of school for the day in Danvers to attend the Special Olympics.

Sheila — "The school was very understanding."

Alex also had an effect on the Special Olympics. Because his participation had such an impact on the games, they are going to name the Special Olympics in Malden, 'The Alex Games', after Alex.

The event also had a big impact on the lives of the children who participated and their parents. It showed these kids, with Down syndrome, cerebral palsy, and autism, and children like Alex with no diagnosis, that they were just like everybody else. They could be part of the excitement and hear the cheers and adulation of the crowd.

Chapter 13 – Challenger League Baseball

Another significant activity in Alex's life was Challenger League baseball, the Challenger Division of the town's Little Leagues, where he played each Sunday at Forestdale Park.

Marie Shea is the co-founder of Challenger League baseball.

"It started in 2007. We were seeing kids dropping out of regular baseball and Bernie Colbert, who co-founded it with me, had a child who is autistic. He wanted to start a league where his son could play baseball, but didn't want to think it would be just in his name, so we got together to talk about it and I put in the application – that's why he says I started it."

Alex was with them that first year. He was nine years old.

Marie – "Alex was with us for twelve seasons, the entire time we've been operating."

They started out small, with a small number, about fifteen kids, and have grown every year since then.

Marie – "It's a wonderful program to have these kids who can't play regular baseball. The parents are really happy to have a place for their kids to go and play. Just the smile on their faces is enough. They look forward to it all year round. That's what they talk about all winter. When is baseball starting? Just today I got an email from one of the parents. They're looking forward to it, they're asking, 'When's baseball starting?' "

They play at the same field every Sunday afternoon, which was made handicap accessible two years ago. There are four teams, broken up based on severity, the lower teams having the more severe disabilities. Some of the kids are in wheelchairs, some, like Alex, are assisted by a partner. Some parents will ask for their kids to be in a lower team. They usually hit off a tee.

Bernie is the district manager - "Everyone has an assistant, a partner that helps them. They catch the ball for them and hand it to them to throw, and help them walk or wheel to the base."

Marie – "We have what are called buddy-zones. The buddies go out and help with the kids at every game. They work with each kid individually. So if you're assigned as a buddy you're going to be working in the field with that child, working with him at bat. You help him get his helmet on. We try to have them from start to finish work with that buddy."

Marie said that the majority of the time they have enough volunteers to have buddies for every game.

Alex could play the field, though he wasn't too much on defense and didn't have a glove. He used the walker to move to the base. Playing in the league was fun, but what Alex liked even more was Challenger Day.

Ron Giovino is the founder of the Medford Invitational Tournament or MIT.

Bernie Colbert — "I've been friends with Ron for twenty years He's there every Sunday for the games. He jumped right in and volunteered, while at the same time running an invitation tournament for the twelve-year-old all star championship league."

Ron — "At the end of the year we'd bring all the little league teams from the cities in the district together into Medford. Then when I started working with and participating with the Challenger League, I thought we should do the same thing with them, so Challenger Day was born."

One day a year after the end of the season and baseball is over, they bring all the Challenger League teams from the surrounding cities together. They started with twenty Special Needs athletes. Now they have seventy-five.

Gary Christianson, Mayor of Malden — "Challenger Day used to be held in Medford. I was so impressed with the event that I began lobbying for it to move to Malden. It worked out where they weren't getting all they felt they should to have a successful event, and I said, then let's do it in Malden."

It's been there ever since.

"I take a lot of grief for that from Medford folks," the mayor said.

Ron - "Each kid plays a one inning game of baseball. We announce the players, play music, have all kinds of celebrities, all the kids have uniforms. There's a lot of support from the city of Malden, and we get a lot of corporate donations, so we're able to spend some serious money on this."

The cities involved include Malden, Billerica, Wakefield, Lynn, and Danvers, and includes kids from the surrounding area that join those leagues. The children really enjoy it, but Bernie thinks the adults enjoy it more.

It wasn't always this way.

Bernie — "When we first started the Challenger League, we really didn't know what to expect. We really didn't know what we were going to see each time we showed up. But after a couple of games the parents would come to us and tell us how much the kids enjoyed it and how much they appreciated everything we were doing. They came and cheered on their children like they would for typical kids. It was very rewarding."

There is no doubt that Alex enjoyed and benefited from the league.

Bernie – "His smile was always there. He'd get excited, you could hear him making noise, his arms would move. He was engaged. Especially on Challenger Day, he loved the music."

Marie – "It was great to see Alex, how he grew with the program. When he first came he was in a wheelchair. Then they took the chair away and his dad used to walk him around the bases. Alex would get to first base and just plop down. Then they got that nice walker for him, and he was proud. He was able to walk around the bases. It was real nice to see how he progressed with the program. Same with the other kids, but Alex was there for twelve years, and you could really see his progression."

Bernie, who has an autistic boy who is now twenty-two, agrees that the program definitely has a positive effect on the kids.

"Their communication skills and eye to eye engagement is improved. If you didn't engage them they would just sit back."

Marie – "Sometimes the kids don't want to do anything. They have to be dragged to the park. Then they get to the field and you see their faces light up. They may not realize it, being Special Needs, that they're going to the field, but once they get there you can see their excitement, especially when they get up to bat. It's a different experience, to hit the ball and everything."

As with anyone playing sports, playing the game gives them a feeling of accomplishment, even Alex. He was obviously progressing and enjoying himself, smiling and having a good time.

Marie – "Alex was there with his dad. They were spending time together. His father was his buddy. He took him around. It was a special time with just the two of them to enjoy."

Jerry told me he enjoyed it as much as Alex did.

Figure 5- Alex and his dad at Devir Park in Malden

Ron – "The other thing with Alex is that every child has a different time slot. Some kids like Alex can't express themselves as well as others, but when Alex was there on the field he would always be fully involved - we would make him be. When he was up to bat and I was pitching to him, I wanted eye contact, and Alex gave me that, and that smirk on his face. And that grew from when he first started with Bernie. When that walker came in he was a changed person."

Alex was fully engaged. He enjoyed being part of a team, just like any other boy. Jerry would be there the whole time, with him on the field, cheering him on.

Ron – "Alex enjoyed Challenger Day. You could see how happy he was. He may not have been as able to express it like some other kids, but we knew Alex, he'd been with us for over a decade, we knew how happy he was. He got more and more engaged. He was one of those kids who grew from the program, so we knew the program worked. I think we all had a strong relationship with Alex."

Alex may have been less than fortunate in some ways, but in others he was extremely blessed. Not only did he have exceptional parents, all these special programs were getting started just as he came on the scene, things like Malden's inclusive PACE program, the Special Olympics, and the Challenger League.

Ron also thinks those non-Special Needs athletes and students who participated and got to work and play with these kids have benefited, too.

Bernie – "We reached out to our local Little Leagues in Malden and Melrose, and they volunteered a team every year to bring their players down and play with our teams. They liked us and we liked them. To see another athlete come down with his hat and his glove and his uniform was exciting for our kids."

They didn't play against the Challenger League teams, but would assist them and be their playing buddies, protecting them.

Bernie – "So if Alex was in the field and a ball[17] was hit to him, his buddy would catch it for him and give it to him to throw."

Ron – "It was wonderful to see how these star athletes were working with these Special Needs kids. The relationship didn't end on the field. The athletes would always say hi to these kids like they would any other baseball players."

Bernie and Marie attest that the City of Malden has been especially supportive.

"Gary, the Mayor, even comes and pitches sometimes," Marie informed me.

---

[17] They play with a very soft safety ball, not a real baseball.

If you ask the parents of the children they have helped over the years or saw the joy on the faces of the young people as they play, you would know what an incredible job Marie, Bernie, and Ron have done in providing a sustaining environment for these children. These people really get it. They show by example how we can share a little of ourselves to make a big difference in the world. By giving Special Needs kids a chance at a regular life, they show they are just like the rest of us. Just as human.

Ron — "Alex was different than most of the kids. His condition was unique. We have autistic, blind, Down syndrome, cerebral palsy, kids with anger and emotional issues. We have it all. Some kids you would look at and say why are you here? All different variations of Special Needs."

Sometimes the unexpected gratitude can be overwhelming.

Bernie — "The first time it happened, we had this girl in a wheelchair, and the first day after the game the mother comes to me and hugged me with tears in her eyes, and thanks me for giving her child something special. I had tears in my eyes, too."

He found his calling.

Not everyone can give their Special Needs child the attention and enjoyment Penny and Jerry gave Alex.

Marie — "Some people come here every weekend to the game and it's a special thing for them to be here. They don't have anything else for their child to do. Some have a single parent and require a twenty-four hour nurse, or are in a wheelchair, but don't have a van. There just aren't that many activities someone like that can participate in."

At the Challenger League, with their buddies, these children are able to do things like the other kids. Everything is geared to their needs. They hit off the tee. Someone runs for them or pushes them around the field.

Marie — "That girl Bernie was talking about is nineteen now, but for her safety she's with the younger age group. We take extra precautions with her. So every weekend she has something to do and participate in with other kids other than going to school. If that doesn't prolong their lives, I don't know what will."

Ron — "It's inspirational for the parents. It gives them courage. That they can affect their children's lives, try to get them that power of socializing. It also allows parents to socialize with each other, as well. It gives them empowerment."

Bernie said that when they first come it's hard to get the kids to go along with what they want them to do. A lot of times they will just refuse to participate, and sit down and not do anything.

Ron – "By the end of the year, if we can get them to focus on one little thing, we're happy, and we have that happen, because at first we couldn't get them to do anything, and each year we get them to do a little more."

Ron went on to describe how, like Alex's teachers and caregivers, they celebrate small victories.

"We had a girl in a wheelchair. One of our coaches, Joe Cappelli, helped her and worked with her all the time. It was her turn to bat and she's never been able to do it before. She's still trying. And Joe said, 'She's going to do it. She's going to do it this time.' She's non-verbal, there's little eye movement, although she does get excited. She has cerebral palsy, one hand that doesn't work, and one twisted that's barely usable. We put the bat in her hand and put the ball on the tee. Joe said, 'She's going to do it by herself, watch.' But she hasn't ever come close, so we're all doubting it. We put her in the right position. Joe said, 'Go ahead, sweet-heart, do it.'

"It was the most emotional, inspirational moment I've seen in my life to see the determination on her face. She struggled to lift that bat, and really just barely touched the ball, knocking it off the T, but the whole crowd exploded with applause and cheers. You'd think she was playing for the Boston Red Sox and just cleared the bases in the bottom of the 9th. It was an incredible moment. You should have seen her glow."

Bernie – "You just kind of learn as you go. The parents were the ones who educate us about their kids. They really do. Special thanks to Penny and Jerry. They did so much."

Challenger League baseball runs from April to the end of June. Registration for the summer is in February, when the kids sign up. There is a web site[18], but usually people just contact Marie for the Challenger League. Ron has a contact for the MCT (Medford Challenger Tournament). They also mention the program to all the different leagues when they have the district meetings, and talk about it so everyone knows.

Challenger League Baseball was one of the best things that ever happened to Alex.

---

[18] On facebook.com/madistrict12Challenger

Chapter 14 – Malden High

One of the most eventful times in Alex's life was when he attended Malden High School, which he did from 2011 to 2018, although he graduated in 2015 with the rest of his class.

It didn't start out smoothly.

Jerry – "When we were thinking about putting Alex in Malden High School, we heard nothing but horror stories about the place and the Special Ed program, about how bad it was. When we got to Malden it turned out to be a fantastic program."

At first there was just a single tiny room, about the size of the average dining room. Before Alex started, however, the single tiny classroom was expanded and enlarged into four bigger ones.

Jerry –"We went in with a lot of trepidation. We had a bad attitude. 'This is a horror show,' I told Veronica, who ran the program. We used to bump heads all the time. One day she said to me, 'Give me a chance. If you don't like it we can talk again, but just give me a chance.' We gave her a chance and it turned out wonderful, phenomenal."

The whole school system was undergoing a profound change in how it handled Special Needs students.

Gary Christenson, the Mayor of Malden - "We have several schools in the city. There's Edrunning Center, Pre-K Five K thru Eights, a separate charter school, the Mystic Valley Regional Charter School, and a private school, the Cheverus, as well as Malden Catholic High School. None of them, except the charter school, have a Special Ed Program, and their Special Needs population was under ten percent."

Gary told us that there were 1842 students at Malden High in 2018, of which 14.1%[19] were Special Needs.

Dana Brown was Principal at Malden High School for thirteen years, from 2003 to 2016.

"It's almost as if Alex and Penny and Jerry were there at this precise time when all of this was getting started, to teach us."

When the principal's job opened in 2003, Dana applied and got the position.

Dana – "It was a remarkable place to be."

---

[19] From https://maldenps.org/high - Malden High School Profile

Dana[20] always thought having Alex at the school was like the hand of Providence working behind the scenes.

"When I look back at it, it was really special, like the hand of God. All these programs and things started just as Alex was coming up through the school system. There are too many coincidences to think it wasn't part of a bigger plan."

When Dana and Alex got there, there were only one and a half class rooms for students with severe special needs. By the time they left there were seven.

Dana – "We made a conscious decision to bring kids back from institutions, group homes, hospitals, and home alone with caretakers. We wanted these students to be physically in our school."

It started in 2011, the same time Alex got there. Dana's philosophy ran counter to many of those in education for a long time, but things are coming around to where Dana thinks it should be.

Dana - "I went out of my way to know as many of the kids as physically possible. To not only know them but know their families as well. Kids would walk down the hall and I would call them by name. They were absolutely flabbergasted that I knew who they were. You do that enough times, you get to know them and their families."

Dana has that crazy ability to remember names and faces. Even today years later, when they come back, he remembers their name.

"You remember me, Mr. Brown?" they'd say.

"Of course, I remember you," he'd reply.

Dana – "I think when you start with personalizing and you know who they are and what their needs are, and who their families are, you can solve a lot of problems. Kids want to come to school, want to tell you things, they want to behave better, you can know a lot, but you have to know them."

The school built new class rooms, PT rooms, and OT rooms[21], with the idea of no longer sending those with special needs away all over the state, but trying to get as many of them as possible back to the high school.

Dana believes it benefited the other students and faculty as much as it did the families and students with special needs.

"Our kids who were not in wheelchairs, who were not with aides or not getting toileted, or didn't have tracheal tube, were learning how

---

[20] Dana is now the principal for Boston Public Schools at the Dearborn School.
[21] Physical Therapy and Occupational Therapy rooms

to behave better, to hold the elevator for a handicapped kid trying to get on, and not pushing kids out of the way. It really benefited the entire school as much as Alex and his family. Looking back, it's amazing the impact this inclusion had."

As it turned out, Alex became sort of an icon around the school.

Dana – "He had celebrity status among the students of Malden High School. High school kids sometimes do things for the right reason, sometimes they do things for the wrong reason, but the kids wanted to be seen with Alex. These are fourteen, fifteen, and sixteen-year-olds. They wanted to be the kid pushing Alex's wheelchair. They wanted to be the one helping him up when he walked."

The same kids, girls mostly, who had been skipping their recess and lunch periods to play with Alex in the Special Needs classrooms since grade school, were still there, now in high school with him. They were now gaining high school credits for their time helping him, although it didn't seem like work to them. They were just having fun with Alex. These friendships persisted right through high school. A few of these girls (see chapter 21) were inspired by their experiences working with Alex to become Special Education teachers themselves.

Alex was not only included, with his dad, he participated big time, taking part in all and every school activity. From plays to recitals, to basketball games and softball tournaments, home and away, Alex and his dad were there. Alex even washed cars at the high school car wash.

Dana – "What I learned early on from Penny and Jerry was that their kid, 'my kid', was going to have the very same experience every other kid at Forestdale or Malden High School had. Their kid was going to take advantage of every single opportunity offered, no questions asked. We want wheelchair access - there were times when we were physically lifting Alex off something, a bleacher or chair, a bench. We weren't going to say Alex can't do this because of his challenges. That was not negotiable."

Alex liked to be around people, and everyone seemed to gather around him and wanted to be with him. Even at the smaller activities, like a poetry reading, where only a few people attended, Alex and his dad were there.

Dana – "I'd go to some events where there'd only be a few people there, and I'd be there, and look around at the audience, and there would be Jerry and Alex. And I'd say, 'Wow, I can't believe he's here.' It just went to prove to me how dedicated they were as parents, and how really rich Alex's life was. He got to go everywhere and was never alone. He enjoyed it."

Jerry – "We went to a school play in Beverly once. We pulled up and started taking Alex out of the van, and five or six people drove up and said they weren't sure they were in the right place. But when they saw me and Alex, they knew they were at the right place."

Everyone knew him.

Dana – "There were four or five families, with Jerry, Alex and me, watching the kids perform in a little play. It was beautiful, and having Jerry and Alex there made it special for everybody."

Alex especially liked the sports events, basketball and football or softball, where there were kids running around the field and people yelling and clapping in the stands.

Alex and his dad were big supporters of the girl's high school softball team, which had a run at the State finals in 2012. He and Jerry went to all the games, home and away. He became the team's number one fan as they won game after game. The girls, some of whom he had known from grade school, made a big deal about him.

Winning the District Championship was quite an achievement. At the award ceremony at the end of the game, Penny, Jerry, and Alex went behind the backstop to watch. Alex was in his chair. There were interviews and group pictures with the coach and the team.

Jerry – "They presented the trophy to John Furlong, the coach, and took pictures of him and the team. Then the media interviewed him. We were watching from behind the backstop. The interviews ended and John looked around and said, 'Where's Alex'. When he spotted Alex, he came right over to him and put the trophy on his lap."

A show of appreciation for what Alex did for the team.

Dana – "The kids stayed with Alex. They thought he was good luck. At the end everyone came over to say hi."

Jerry – "Even when we went to away games at different places, people from the other school, the other teams, couldn't do enough for us. 'Do you want something? Can we get you something? You want a hot dog? You want a drink?' They would come up and say, 'Is he Alex,' and I'd say, 'Yep.'"

Gary Christenson, Mayor of Malden – "Alex and his father had passion for his school and friends. That's something I preach. I wish we had more pride in this fast-paced world that we live in. Alex and Jerry had that and that's what drew me to them. They were engaged."

I asked Jerry why he took Alex to all the school events. He of course said, he did it for Alex and his friends. On closer questioning, however, it turned that he did it for himself, as well. It made him feel good to see how everyone reacted to Alex and made him feel a part of things. He felt proud, both of Alex and his friends. It was a wonderful thing to see.

Dana – "I didn't really figure it out until Jerry brought Alex to a girl's basketball game one day. As an educator, I was trying to understand how much a young student like Alex understands? How much could he process with his disability? My goodness, he was following the ebb and flow of the game, rocking back and forth with excitement. He knew what was going on. We don't have to figure it out for him."

Same thing with music - Jerry and Penny would take Alex to the school concerts, or to a chorus or the band rehearsal, and he would bounce to the rhythm. He reacted to the music just like anyone would.

Dana – "He knew which songs were upbeat and which were soft or slow. So that's when I realized as an educator that these kids are part of things."

In his senior year, 2015, Alex participated in several big events. One was the Annual Senior Fashion Show.

Jerry – "We asked if Alex could be in the fashion show. They told us that all the tuxedos had already been donated."

They suggested that Jerry go to Men's Wearhouse and talk to them about donating another tux.

Jerry – "The store told us that they had already donated their quota, but made an exception for Alex. He went in and they measured him for one."

Alex was the only participant accompanied by not one, but two beautiful girls, Elyse and Christina Valente. Elyse was a senior. Her older sister, Christina, had graduated the previous year.

Figure 6 - Alex with Elyse and Christina Valente at the Fashion Show

Another noteworthy event occurred early that year, when Alex received the "Honorary Mr. Malden High Award', an award handed out by the students annually.

Jerry – "They have this Mr. Malden High competition every year. It's kind of like Miss America, but for boys. They have a swim suit competition, and have them dressed up in tuxedos and things. We stopped by to see the show. They had five competitors, and we asked if there was anything we could do. They asked us if Alex had a suit and we said yes. They told us to bring his walker and suit, and follow them backstage."

They wanted Alex to help hand out the awards. At the intermission they came and got him.

Jerry – "The show went on, and at the end of the show, after the winner had been selected, at the voting, they presented the Honorary Mister Malden High School award to Alex. He came out to a standing ovation. We were completely surprised."

The students themselves decided to award the trophy to Alex.

Figure 7- Alex voted Honorary Mister Malden High

The most important event that year was graduation, which was held outside at the football stadium, where he would walk up the aisle with the other students to get his diploma.

Jerry – "We went to the rehearsal to try it. They had the whole graduating class walk past the grandstand from one end of the field to the other, then circle back and walk up the other side of the field about halfway. Then they marched back across toward the viewing stand and took their seats."

But Alex couldn't do it. It was too far for him to walk and he was holding up the line.

Jerry – "I told Mister Mastrangelo, the house principal, 'This isn't working.' "

The principal agreed, and Jerry came up with a new idea.

Jerry - "They had Alex sit at the end of the field where the line turned to cross to the other side and double-back. When the line reached him, Alex got up and walked to his seat with the other kids with no problem. When they called his name, he walked up and got his diploma like everyone else."

His teacher, Rachel, was with him helping him walk. His proud parents sat in the audience. For Penny and Jerry, who had dedicated their lives to Alex and watched him overcome so much, seeing him in his gown with all the other kids, walking up to get his diploma, was the most overwhelming, rewarding experience of their lives. They wept freely with joy.

Penny – "My brothers Jimmy and Joey were there with us. We all cried."

Mr.Brown and Me

Figure 8 - Alex receiving his high school diploma (Special Needs) from Mr. Brown

Dana – "Alex's participation meant a lot to everyone in the high school. He was literally the mayor of Malden High. It was like he was prom king, the star athlete, the class president, all in one, because of his personality, his grin, his smile. He was everywhere, in the hallway, in the gym, at the cafeteria, the main office to see me. People knew who he was."

Jerry – "Alex would walk down the halls and randomly go into the class rooms. Everyone would say 'Hi, Alex!' "

Even though there were half a dozen 'Alexs' in the school, everyone knew who you were talking about when you said his name.

Dana – "They knew that not only did he have his mother and father behind him, but there was a whole team of people, Team Alex, mostly pretty girls. He had strong support and wonderful educators over the course of this time. It was hard to describe. I think of this fifteen year period, and think of what had happened in Malden High School over this time, there's just too many coincidences for me to think it was haphazard, just an accident."

Gary Christianson– "Alex spent as much time with the school as I did when I was there, not just what he had to do to graduate, but at all the different events in the school calendar outside the regular school day. Alex was definitely a big part of the school."

Jerry and Penny made it that way.

The Malden school system went through an astounding change in the fifteen years Alex was there. He, as much as Dana or the teachers, was responsible for much of this growth.

Dana – "We spend so much time worrying about test scores and accountability and measuring the school by xyz. Truth be told, when I got there most white middle class parents were not sending their kids to Malden High School. They considered it to be a bad school. There were a lot of fights and discipline issues, a lot of negative publicity around the school. We changed that. It took us a number of years to change it where people felt comfortable sending their kids there, but we did it because we got to know the kids and their families.

"I think the greatest thing someone ever said to me, it was a young lady, she said, 'We like you here because we feel safe with you here.' I thought about that sixteen-year-old, with all the things they think about in their lives, that my impact on her was that she felt safe in the school when I was there. Made me think, wow, think about it, school can be a scary place.

"Not that it was all rosy. There were some tough moments, because some didn't want to buy into the idea that school is a good place to be. We don't come here to cause disruptions and chaos, but to learn and grow and help others do the same. Turning desks upside down and making fun of others is not the way to succeed."

Dana continued.

"We strive for a good solid school, where everyone is on a path to something, but there were outliers who didn't believe in this."

Dana said discipline wasn't the answer.

Dana – "It took me a long time to change, but what I realized was that throwing kids out, walking kids out, suspending them for thirty days, doing all that only had a short term impact."

He realized that discipline alone had no long term effect in changing behavior.

Dana – "Believe it or not, some of our malcontents and disgruntled kids, who didn't know what they were doing at high school, when kids like that volunteered for Special O, or going down to Unified Sports (see Chapter 16), pushing a wheelchair and helping kids up, they finally got it. The light bulb went off, now they know why we're all here! The best way to show people what to do is by example."

When Alex was using his walker or was going somewhere, it wasn't unusual for Dana to throw out his arm for Alex to grab and they'd walk together.

Dana – "So when the principal walks down the hall with Alex, or pushes his chair, that's OK, it must be the right thing to do. This is good. I can't do it every minute of every day, but I did it enough times so that people realized that Alex is a student at Malden High School, period, end of discussion. Alex is a student of Malden High School, he's one of us.

"If you really want to promote your school as being an all-inclusive school, as being a good school, you've got to walk the walk. A number of people did, but in some cases the kids led the way. Special Olympics, Unified Sports, Challenger Baseball, there was a core group of adults who made it happen. But there also were a lot of kids who helped open our eyes and made you say, this is pretty good.

"I think there were times I was criticized at Malden High because I treated the sad sacks as well as I treated the kids who were going to BC. I like the underdogs. I like the kids who are a pain in the butt, who some of the other teachers didn't like. Those were the ones who had to come to my office for a snack. I like that type of kid."

Malden High was extreme. Even Dana wasn't ready for the severity of many of the Special Needs children's disabilities.

"When I taught in Chelsea and Lynnfield, I didn't see the type of Special Needs students I would see when I got to Malden. When I talk to other principals around the State, they don't understand the depth of what you're dealing with in a full inclusive school. We had a kid with a trach-tube, another with her heart growing outside her body[22], and some like Alex.

Alex was not the only one to benefit from going to Malden High.

Paula, Penny's next door neighbor – "I loved Malden High. I was in Class of '82. My kids went to Catholic school, Hannah, until the 8th grade. When Nicole graduated 8th grade she wanted to go to the local Catholic high school. She insisted on going there. It was a big mistake. Hannah just thrived at Malden High. Nicole had a terrible time at the Catholic school."

Paula can't say enough about Malden High, its diversity, the lack of racism.

Paula - "It's just amazing to see all types of people together. Look how they treated Alex, he was surrounded by love there. I mean the kids just adored him. No one discriminated there. It tells you a lot about the teachers and parents. Alex was accepted for who he was at Malden High School."

Gary Christenson, the Mayor – "I graduated there in 1986 and comparing it to today, I think the school's been one of our city's major strength. It was there that I knew I wanted to be mayor and they helped prepare me to get there. And I see that in a lot of our students today. So there's something about Malden High that really does help prepare students for what they want to achieve in life."

Alex certainly benefitted from going there.

---

[22] Her heart is outside her chest. She is now over twenty-two years old.

Chapter 15 – A Special Ed Teacher

One of the people most involved with Alex while he was at the high school was his Special Ed teacher, Rachel Hanlon.

Rachel – "I met Alex in 2013. He was in a different class, but they were thinking of moving him to my class to be with his friend, James, who was being moved up. They were good buddies, so it was beneficial to keep them together."

James and Alex sat together and had known each other since grade school.

Rachel – "James would wait for Alex to arrive, and when the Gentiles' car drove up, James would wait by the door in his wheelchair. They sat together everyday at lunch. Alex had the biggest reaction with James. He would always smile when he saw James."

Alex moved to Rachel's class in the middle of the 2014 school year, when he was seventeen. He was in one of six classrooms (now five) with thirty to forty students in all. Rachel's class was for 12th grade to twenty-two-year-olds. Alex could use a walker by that time and had learned to walk. Penny and Jerry observed the class and had to approve the move, which they did.

Rachel grew up and went to school in Connecticut. She graduated and went to Smith College in North Hampton, Massachusetts, with a minor in Elementary Education. She hadn't intended to get into Special Ed.

Rachel – "In a College assignment I tutored and worked with a Special Needs child, a third grader, who had ADHD (Attention Deficit/Hyper active). It was a great experience."

She also worked a few summers at Day Care in her hometown with a Special Needs twelve-year-old boy, who really connected with her.

"He was very cooperative and would seek me out."

In her senior year of college, Rachel began looking for work. She went to a job fair and applied at a school in Southborough dedicated to kids with autism – New England Center for Children - which had a graduate program. She got the job.

Rachel – "I started thinking back on all these experiences with Special Needs kids and thought I'd give it a try and fell in love with it. I got my Masters degree in Special Ed, specializing in autism. The school paid 80% of the cost of my degree. I was there three years."

Rachel told me that the gender mix with autism is about 3-1 male to female.

She learned about the different types of disabilities, Down syndrome, autism, cerebral palsy, etc., and the strategies to deal with each one, as well as the types of assessments.

"I was taught how to assess each one, how to differentiate the types of disabilities, concentrating on autism in a school that specialized in it."

But Alex was different from the types of disability Rachel learned about in college.

Rachel – "Alex was a whole new experience from what I had been doing. I was never exposed to kids like Alex. It made me go back to basics and re-approach the problem. For three years I had used the same approach (as she had for autism). Going to Malden and seeing kids like Alex changed everything. I had to reassess everything."

She researched Alex's condition and found that it was relatively rare. There was not much written about it. She also learned that more than half of those with his disability didn't live past twenty-five. She thought Alex was going to be one of those who beat the odds because of his determination.

"Alex was a fighter," she told me. "So were Penny and Jerry. You can't let the odds like this defeat you. I thought sure they would defeat the odds."

Penny and Jerry intimidated her at first. They had a reputation for being aggressive and very involved, for speaking up on Alex's behalf.

Rachel – "Many parents are not as involved. Many are more passive and leave things to us. Jerry and Penny always pushed for more, never content to accept things. They would push to have us try different speech therapies and devices, for more physical training and therapy."

As a Special Needs teacher, she would much rather have involved parents than passive ones, even though it can be more challenging.

Rachel – "Penny and Jerry were constantly challenging us to do more."

Rachel confirmed that many of the students at Malden High wanted to come in and work with the Special Needs class.

"They interacted directly with the kids, coloring with them, reading to them, talking to them. It started out informally at Forestdale, with kids going there instead of recess or lunch, but ended allowing students to get credit for working with a teacher in their classroom, doing clerical tasks mostly, making copies and things like that.

"It was so encouraging to see all these students come and help the kids, young people with such a sense of compassion and service to others, boys as well as girls. One of the boys who volunteered, Joe 'Tag', who was on the football team, now works as a para."

Some of the kids said that this program[23] changed their thoughts about kids with disabilities, and made them consider going into the Special Ed field. They realized that the Special Needs kids are just like everyone else.

Rachel had Alex for four years.

"He was in the more active class."

They worked on recognizing numbers and faces, which he seemed poor in, and working on his stamina, which improved. There was also vocational training, such as packaging food, putting cans of juice in plastic bags.

Rachel – "In the beginning it was hard to get him to focus. He would keep dropping the bag or ignoring it."

Alex was eventually able to do this.

Rachel – "When he was in a good mood, he would work and push to get it done, but he could be stubborn, challenging. He had a will."

A lot of the exercises for the active class were for strengthening and keeping them on the go. They did things like stand at the table for a minute, which Alex did well.

Rachel – "Alex was a happy kid. He would smile a lot and didn't necessarily have to be coaxed to do so, just spontaneously. The best days were when he would break into a big belly laugh. He had the greatest belly laugh."

Alex responded to things around him and was observant. He liked water and meadows.

Rachel – "Alex reacted to what was going on. He knew a lot more than people gave him credit for."

Alex couldn't verbalize, but had his way of letting you know what he wanted.

Rachel – "Alex would grab my hand when he wanted me to tickle him."

Rachel resigned from Malden High in 2018 to become Special Needs Team Chair for the Arlington Elementary School's

---

[23] The School to Career Program

Individualized Education Program (IEP). This is open to any child with Special Needs. They work on goals and objectives to achieve the best results for the students, most of whom are in regular class rooms. They meet once a year to assess the child. This program involves two elementary schools, both with separate inclusion programs.

Rachel – "The goal of this program is to put the kids in the least restrictive environment, versus restrictive environments like I taught at for three years, where everyone there is autistic and they live right at the school. Malden is in between, with separate classes for Special Needs, but inclusive cafeteria and Unified Sports."

When asked what she would tell parents of a Special Needs child like Alex, she said, "Don't give up."

Her advice was to learn as much as you can about your child and his or her condition. Know what's available for services and support, and don't be afraid to ask for it.

Rachel – "People with special needs are just like you and me. They may need a little help to get through the day. Don't be afraid to spend time with them. You might learn something about yourself and find it a very rewarding experience."

Rachel believes that neglecting children like this and putting them away in institutions and hospitals should be a thing of the past. She hopes to be able to get these kids the best help available. It helps that there is now mandated reporting of abuse and neglect. Institutionalizing is becoming less common nowadays.

Rachel – "Kids slip through the cracks, but it's easier to get support now, than to not."

Educators have to be watchful of their students' behavior and know the signs of neglect, abuse, and lack of nutrition.

Rachel told me that families move to Malden specifically for the Special Needs program. As we have seen, Malden is inclusive on several levels.

Rachel – "Malden is one of the most diverse cities in the country."

The races are mixed - Asian, Hispanic, African American, Middle Eastern.

Rachel - "I taught Chinese, Mexicans, Haitians, Moroccans."

There were several different languages spoken at the high school when Rachel was there.

Rachel – "Going there was an eye-opener. I learned to appreciate the diversity."

One of Rachel's biggest challenges as a Special Ed teacher was a very smart, unpredictable autistic child, who learned how to thwart and sabotage her every attempt to teach him anything. Alex wasn't like that, but presented challenges of his own.

Rachel — "He had so many limitations that it was difficult to determine goals and objectives, but he was also the most rewarding, because when you did achieve something, it made it that much more meaningful. We would celebrate the small gains."

There are other rewards. Parents show appreciation when you make a change for the better in their child's life.

Rachel — "Sometimes things can be difficult and you don't see any results, and you think you're not being effective and feel like you should just quit. But the next day you see some gain in a pupil, someone says, thank you, or, as with Alex, you get a smile, then it's all worth it."

Chapter 16 – Unified Sports

One of the more noteworthy aspects of the high school, indicative of the school's inclusive policy, is Unified Sports.

Dana – "It was started by Barbara Scibelli, who worked in the office at the high school, and the Captain's Club, where top athletes teamed up to work with Special Needs kids. In many ways, it was an offshoot of the Malden Special Olympics.

"After we established the Malden Day Games and the Special Olympics, we asked, 'What are we doing during the school day?' So we came up with the idea of unified sports."

The idea is to match up Special Needs students with regular ability students, many of them student athletes. They all have a gym class together at a regular time and play sports. In kickball, which is played in the gym, the typical-ability kid kicks the ball and wheels or walks the Special Needs boy or girl to the base.

Dana – "I get goose bumps just thinking about it, because the impact it had on the regular students is just as great as it was on Alex and his family. A whole generation of Malden High School kids has a far greater understanding of what it means to support someone with medical needs or mental health issues."

They had students with depression and anxiety, in wheelchairs, and kids with trach-tubes. There was a whole range of special needs and typical ability students. Those kids who could walk and talk and run grew and developed from the experience just as much as Alex and his Special Needs classmates did.

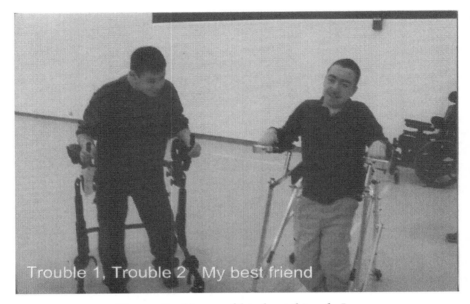

Trouble 1, Trouble 2, My best friend

Figure 9- Alex and his best friend, James

"It really took off," said Dana.

Unified Sports became part of the fabric of Malden high to the point where it's now part of the curriculum, an official course in the program of studies that students register and get credit for.

Dana — "When we started it was this little ad hoc program. We'd ask kids, 'Hey, you want to be part of Unified Sports? Show up everyday at period three.'"

Unified Sports is a national program. The Massachusetts State Athletic Department for high schools has adapted Unified Sports as their standard. They have their own track meets. In schools like Malden High it has become a way of life, though there are still a lot of high schools that have yet to adopt it.

Dana — "It's a big commitment in costs as well as time. However, it's gaining traction as more and more schools join the bandwagon, just as they have the Special Olympics that were started fifty years ago."

Rachel, Alex's high school teacher, remembers Unified Sports well.

"The students led the gym class. It was great to see school athletes working with the Special Needs kids, with stretching and exercising. They played games like kickball and volleyball."

82

It taught the regular kids leadership skills. They learned about disabilities and differences, how we are all the same, to be appreciative. The Special Needs kids learned social skills and gained mobility.

Rachel – "Alex hated stretching. He did standing exercises with another student. Alex, because of his severe handicap, always partnered with a teacher. He couldn't really play volleyball, so when they did that Alex did bowling or the beanbag toss. He played kickball. He could kick the ball and use his walker to get to first base. Students would take him on laps around the gym. Alex loved the Unified Sports class."

Friendships were made. In Alex's last year of high school, a fifteen-year-old sophomore named Josh teamed with him.

Rachel – "They would sit and talk. Alex would always smile when Josh came in."

Figure 10 - Alex and his friend, Josh

Another one of those participating with Alex in Unified Sports was Alyssa Figueiredo, Alex's friend from Forestdale Elementary.

"I don't remember when I first met Alex. I've known him all my life. We went to elementary school and high school together, with Aryzona and Sam (see Chapter 21). We're all in the same grade as Alex."

They would go to the Special Needs classroom(s) during lunch and recess.

Alyssa – "We'd go down together as a group. That's what we did. I heard the girls talking about it one day and decided to go, too. We were all part of Team Alex in the Special Olympics during middle school."

Alyssa has a younger cousin who has special needs and from knowing him and Alex, is used to it and not uncomfortable.

"I would walk Alex around the track for unified gym time. We took turns with him."

Alex also participated in Unified Band and Chorus. The kids went to the band room, where they could hit piano keys and triangles and bang the drums.

The Unified Sports program benefited all who took part in it, typical kids and those with special needs. It certainly had a unifying effect on Malden High.

Chapter 17 – Disney World

All the while Alex was attending school in Malden, he and his family were going on one adventure after another. His parents took him everywhere. One of their favorite places to go was Disney World in Orlando, Florida.

Jerry – "We must have gone there at least twenty times."

They went once a year, sometimes more, every year. Their first visit was in 2003, when Alex was six.

Jerry – "We always tried to go on his birthday, or Christmas, or Halloween, when there was a lot happening. On Halloween we would always dress up. We got phenomenal treatment!"

If not, somebody would hear about it.

Jerry – "Alex would always perk up at the airport in Orlando when we got there. His face would light up and he'd clap when we drove into the parking lot at Disney."

Penny – "In Alex's mind, everyone and everything was there to entertain him."

And Disney World is the entertainment center of the cosmos. They paid full price to get in and it was worth it.

Jerry – "Almost all the facilities, attractions, and rides are handicapped accessible, and everyone is extremely helpful."

The Disney characters would always come over and spend time with Alex, especially Mickey, who always took a picture with him.

Jerry – "Alex was always singled out of the crowd, for some reason. People volunteered to push his wheelchair and things. Once we were there and we got individual pictures with four of the characters, Mickey, Minnie, Goofy, and Donald Duck. When we were finished, Minnie said, 'Wait a minute,' and disappeared around the corner. Then she came back with the other three characters. We got a group picture with all four of them."

Getting a group picture with four main Disney Characters is very rare, but it was an almost everyday occurrence for Alex.

Jerry, Penny, and Alex would meet their old friend from the Malden Bank, Dave Bugden, his wife, Lisa, and their son, Ben, who's fourteen. They all know and love the park as much as the Gentiles do and had great times there together.

The people at Disney really knew how to take care of Alex and his parents.

Jerry – "One night we went to dinner late at the African Lodge in Animal Kingdom and realized that the menu wasn't suitable for Alex. It was too spicy, a weird, different cuisine. So we got on the bus to try and find another place to eat at the Magic Kingdom. It was late by now. We told the bus driver our situation. He said, 'Don't worry' and got on his radio. Then he made a detour and took us to the Wave, where we had a great dinner."

Penny – "Alex ate sushi."

Life seemed good, then something happened that threaten to destroy their world.

On August 31, 2008, after a routine doctor's appointment, Penny was diagnosed with breast cancer. Although it was a shock at first, Penny remained undaunted. Her only concern was taking care of Alex. The fact that he still needed her was all she was concerned about.

Penny was admitted to the hospital and surgery was scheduled. The night before the operation, when Jerry was about to take Alex home for the evening without, 'Mommy', Alex became upset. She explained to him that she had to stay overnight and would see him in the morning. Alex seemed to understand. He calmed down and kissed her good-bye.

After the surgery, Penny underwent radiation and three months of chemo. She lost her hair and became sick.

Penny – "Some days I felt sick after chemo and couldn't do things with Alex. That bothered me more than anything."

As usual, Penny got a lot of support from family and friends. Emily, who babysat for Alex occasionally, moved in with them for awhile to help. One friend, Sheila Krupcheck, made a collection of colorful scarves for Penny. She wore them all over town. People, strangers mostly, who saw her and Alex, would always wave.

Penny – "One day I was driving through town wearing one of the scarves. People waved at us. Then Alex pulled the scarf off my head and laughed. I laughed, too."

Penny insists she was never optimistic. She just didn't consider anything but taking care of Alex. It kept her focused on something positive. His smile and laughter kept her going. Alex was the best medicine. He gave her something to live for.

She was lucky they caught the cancer early and that she had great doctors.

The Gentiles had planned a trip to Disney World for Christmas, and as the time of the planned trip drew close, Penny finally made the decision that she was going to go.

Penny – "I wasn't going to miss it or let Alex miss it just for chemo!"

Two days before Christmas she told her doctors. They were all alarmed, concerned about the large crowds of people with Penny's weakened immune system. She insisted, and they rescheduled the Chemo for her.

That Thursday, immediately after her treatment, she joined Jerry at the airport and flew to Orlando. It worked out that she returned just in time for her next session. As usual, they had a wonderful time. Seeing her child's joy was a tonic stronger than any chemo, and after eight months of treatment, Penny was found to be cancer free.

Kathy Bebo, my wife, spent time with Penny during these months.

"Penny's personality never changed. She was the same sweet, good-natured, upbeat person as always. She didn't get depressed or mad. She didn't skip a beat."

One time they went 'Princess Character Dining' at the Royal Banquet Hall in the Norway pavilion at Epcot. They supped on tasty Norwegian specialties, while the princesses, Snow White, Ayora, Cinderella, and Ariel, walked around the room and talked to people. One of them, Princess Ariel, a pretty redhead, stopped at Penny and Jerry's table and asked if she could feed Alex. The question surprised them. No one had ever asked that before, but they said, go ahead. She fed Alex, wiping his mouth with a napkin. She told them she worked with Special Needs children. Alex smiled for her. I would have smiled, too. When the princesses paraded around the room with the kids, Princess Ariel pushed Alex's chair as she walked.

Disney was like family for the Gentiles, a place of friendly people and warm greetings. One time they were waiting in line to get their pictures taken with some Disney characters. As they came to the first photo shoot area the man standing there to help them said to Alex, "Look who's back!" This was their first visit of the year, and even though they returned often to take pictures when visiting, they hadn't been there since the previous year. Jerry asked him how he remembered them and the man said, "From last year." It made Jerry feel like he had come home.

Figure 11 - Jerry, Alex, and Penny at Disney World

However, all was not a bed of roses. Accidents can still happen, even with the best of precautions. On a recent trip to Disney World, while on the Jungle Cruise, disaster struck.

They were sitting in the boat at the dock waiting to cast off, when a large speaker fell from the ceiling and hit Alex on the head. Luckily, it was a glancing blow, but no one knew that at the time.

Jerry freaked out and ran for Alex, yelling for attention. They had to wait until all the other people were let off the boat before Alex could be taken off. Penny and Jerry didn't know how bad Alex was hurt. It was nerve wracking. Then, after waiting for everyone to disembark, the pilot wanted to move the boat to another location.

Jerry yelled, "Don't move the boat! Get him off!"

The ambulance drove up a minute later and they finally took Alex off.

Penny – "It was quite a crash, and made a large bump. They took Alex to the Disney Hospital[24] in an ambulance, but he was all right."

It was a close call, but other than the bump on the head Alex was all right, although they weren't sure until he could be examined by a doctor.

Disney took care of everything.

The Magic Kingdom was truly a magical place for Alex and his parents. Of all the places they visited over the years, it was Alex's favorite spot.

---

[24] This is the Celebration Hospital, funded and built by Disney.

Chapter 18 – Alex Gets Around

Disney was not the only place Penny and Jerry took Alex. They also went to all the local amusement parks in the area, most of them at least once a year. As they had vowed when they learned about Alex's condition and dedicated their lives to him, every place they went, Alex would also go.

Jerry – "Alex can't go on the rides, but likes to be walked around. He loved people and the lights, to be where there is a lot of action."

They visited Sesame Place, in Langhorne, Pennsylvania, Canobie Lake, in Salem, New Hampshire, and Lake Compounce, as well as the Mystic Aquarium in Connecticut.

Jerry – "We went to Six Flags, in Agawam, a suburb of Springfield, Massachusetts, when we got free tickets once."

They also visited Sea World and Universal Studios when they were in Orlando. They got a discount - Alex went for free, while one of them paid half price.

"It was a good deal," Jerry confirmed. "It's a policy they had for Special Needs kids and their parents."

They also went see Blue Man Group for Alex's eighteenth birthday.

Besides their visits to Disney World in Orlando, they went to Disney on Ice whenever it was in town every year at Christmas and February vacation. Alex loved to watch his favorite characters glide across the ice.

Jerry – "I used to take Alex to the mall all the time, parks, any outdoor activity."

Alex especially liked the mall during Christmas time when there were a lot of people and lights.

Alex loved traffic.

"He loved riding in the car," Jerry told me.

They would get in the van and go for drives along unknown roads for hours.

In 2011 and 2012 Penny and Jerry became involved with the Starlight Foundation, an organization that brought kids around to different events in the city. In July 2011, Alex went on the Duck Tour on the Charles River, where he got to drive the boat. In October of that year he was at the New England Aquarium. That December Alex went to a Christmas party at Jillian's in Boston, bowling, and sat on

Santa's lap. On Christmas Eve Alex went to a private showing of the Muppets, with Bruin player[25], Shawn Thornton (#22). Alex has an autographed picture of Shawn and his autographed Bruins shirt.

Again with the Starlight Foundation, the following year, in July, he went to York Wild Kingdom, a park and zoo in Maine, with a free day pass, although they had to get there on their own.

In September of 2013 they decided to go on their own into Boston to attend opening day of the Rose F. Kennedy Greenway Carousel. Designed by Jeff Briggs, it has fourteen seats, all designed as different kinds of odd creatures - skunks, butterflies, owls, a grasshopper, squirrel, and Right whale, enough for thirty-six riders. Even more unusual, it has three animals (seven seats) for Special Needs children.

Alex is mentioned in an article in the Sunday Globe about the opening.

Boston Globe - *Alex, who is seventeen and can't speak, was in a wheelchair. He smiled at his mother as the carousel spun, and showered his father with kisses between rides. Penny Gentile – "We found out that the carousel had a handicap-accessible ride, then we found out it had three. There are not many parks for him. Some places aren't even handicap accessible, period!"*

The article goes on to mention his MECP2 gene issue, which produces excess proteins, disrupting the nerve cells in the brain and causing developmental disabilities.

Penny – "Alex rode a rabbit with a carrot in its mouth, and the chariot and the rocking boat with serpent-like oarfish. He liked the seal the best because he got to look around at the colors and people."

---

[25] The year they won the Stanley Cup.

Figure 12 - Alex and Jerry on the Rose F. Kennedy Greenway Carousel

In 2014, they put Alex in the van and went to Batting Camp Day at Fenway Park, with the Boston Red Sox. They were part of a caravan carrying twenty kids and ten adults from Malden's Challenger League.

They got T-shirts and tickets for the game later that evening (Yankees vs. Red Sox), and had a visit to the dugout, where they met hitting coach, Victor Rodriguez. They also got to go to the batting tunnel and hit off a tee. Alex met and had a picture taken with Ben Affleck. There were group photos at the warning track, hitting instructions at the home plate batting cage, and a tour of the park. Lunch was in the dugout with Wally, who scared Alex at first. Miraculously, the dugout was clean. No spit!

All of the kids, including Alex, were on the field for Red Sox batting practice that evening and got to watch the game from special seats close to the action. Alex, as usual, cheered for each team as they went out on the field. One woman, an obvious Red Sox fan and unaware of his condition, kept trying to tell him not to cheer for the Yankees! But Alex would have nothing of it, and kept cheering for both teams when they came on.

This was not their first visit to Fenway Park. They had been going to Red Sox games at least once or twice annually for ten years.

Jerry – "The first game we ever went to, as we were leaving, we stopped and talked to a girl in a Red Sox truck. She gave us her number and told us to call next time we went to a game. We called before our next visit and she met us at the park and took us down to the field for batting practice. Alex always got the VIP treatment after that."

Penny – "One of my favorite times was when my dad went with us. It was great seeing Alex and his Papa watching the game together."

Alex's parents made sure he got plenty of activity, even more than most typical kids. Halloween at Salem was always a big treat. Alex loved the commotion. They always dressed up in costumes and joined the throng.

Figure 13 - Jerry, Alex, and Penny on the way to Salem on Halloween

93

Jerry — "Every year on July 3rd we'd go to the Liberty Mutual Preview of the July 4th Pops, outdoors at the Esplanade. They have a special section with handicap seats."

They went to the Nutcracker Suite Ballet in Boston every Christmas they didn't go to Disney.

Jerry — "They really knew how to handle Special Needs people. They had a section off to the left with space for Alex with seats on both sides of him for Penny and me."

On one vacation with Alex they went to Myrtle Beach.

Penny — "Alex didn't seem to care for the beach much at first, until we found a wheelchair for him. It was a special chair built for the beach with big-balloon tires. He sat on the shore. It was an unusual looking chair made from PCV piping, and attracted a lot of attention. People all came over to say hi to Alex."

They went to the Macy's Thanksgiving Parade in Manhattan twice, when Alex was ten and eleven years old.

Jerry — "We went to see them blow up the giant balloons. The cab let us off several blocks from the place because of the crowds, so I went up to a cop and told him where we were going and asked him how to get there."

When the cop saw Alex, he opened the gate blocking off the road and took them down the empty street to the spot they needed to go.

Afterward, as they looked for a cab in the crowded streets to take them back to the hotel, Jerry decided to walk a couple of blocks away and then try to flag one down.

Jerry — "I saw a cop on the corner. Another tourist tried to flag down a cab on the corner and the cop yelled at him. I went up to copy and asked where we could get a cab."

When the policeman saw Alex he said, "Right here", but when Jerry tried to flag one down, the officer told him to stop. Then he pointed to a cab on the street and blew his whistle. It stopped right there on the spot and they were able to get in.

Things like this happened everywhere they went in the City. Some people and places really get it.

One unforgettable day, Penny, Jerry, and Alex went to see the Ringling Brothers' Circus at Boston Gardens. Before the show the circus let people go down to the floor where the ring is to talk to the clowns and meet some of the performers and animals. When Jerry asked the attendant how to get there he took them to a freight elevator and brought them down.

Jerry – "The elevator doors opened and there in front of us, not ten feet away, were these big cats in cages."

The elevator let them out in the staging area where all the circus people gather and eat before the show, including the animals. The attendant brought them out to the ring and told Jerry he'd be watching, and to raise his hand when they wanted to leave. He'd come and take them back.

Jerry – "When we wanted to go back to our seats, I raised my hand and the guy came back and led us out the way we came. We walked out a curtain and there were two gigantic elephants standing right in front of us, unchained, just a few feet away. I was shocked. We stopped dead and stared."

The elephant trainer was surprised too, and said, "Danger, danger!" crossing his arms back and forth in front of him. Cages of big cats and lines of performers stood behind the elephants, ready to start the parade. They scooted passed the line as quick as they could, and went back to the elevator, not a little shaken. It was an encounter Jerry will never forget.

Penny, Jerry, and Alex went out to restaurants to eat almost every night. Kowloon, the large, popular Chinese restaurant on Route 1 in Saugus, was a perennial favorite.

Jerry – "They always made a big deal for Alex. We never had to wait, even when the place was full. On New Years Eve, the busiest night of the year, they would see us and walk us right in through the crowd to be seated."

At Paparazzi's on Clarendon St. in Boston, they have Alex's picture hanging on the wall.

Penny – "The first picture they had on the wall was at five years old. They updated it every year until he was seventeen."

They went there all the time. Waiters and customers would recognize Alex from his picture and ask how he got his face on the wall.

Penny – "He was a celebrity."

At Brutole, an Italian restaurant in Danvers, they were again, always seated regardless of the crowd.

Jerry - "When we walked in they would say, 'Oh, here's our next reservation', and usher us right in."

Spinelli's in East Boston always made the character cakes for Alex's birthday, any character they asked for, including Mickey Mouse and Pooh.

Next door neighbor, Paula English – "I've watched Alex over the years with the wheelchair and the walker. I think that a lesser well-taken care of child with Alex's disabilities would not have progressed as well. It's testament to them as parents. There was never a 'you can't' with them. Never a 'you'll never', or 'you won't' with them. Graduate kindergarten, graduate elementary school, go to the prom, graduate high school, the Olympics, Disney World, all those things we take for granted and Alex did them all. On prom night, I'll never forget it, and in his Halloween costumes, every Halloween. Alex did everything. He did it all."

One wonders how Penny and Jerry could do it. It all seems overwhelming. It would probably not have been possible without the van.

Jerry – "The first thing we did when we learned about Alex's condition was to buy a van."

They had dedicated their lives to Alex, and were determined to take him with them wherever they went. To accomplish this they realized that they would need the proper wheels. One of the first things they did after buying the van was teach Alex how to get in and out of it.

Penny – "It took a lot of effort and planning to take Alex with us everywhere, a lot of heavy lifting."

If you've ever taken your nine-month-old baby out for the day, you might have some idea of the preparation required. It can be a difficult proposition. You need to bring extra sets of clothing, and make sure you have changing places. You have to lift and carry them at times, even if they have a chair. Those who have traveled with someone in a wheelchair know the effort and care needed to do so safely.

As difficult as taking Alex everywhere was, Penny and Jerry found it easy to do. They didn't feel they had to overcome anything. It was easy for them because they had been doing it since Alex was a baby, and they continued to do it. Things that seem hard to others become simple when it's routine, something done every day. A farm lad, who lifts a calf everyday, will be able to lift it when it's full-grown. Penny and Jerry had an everyday routine and Alex fit right into it. It made everything seem easy.

96

There was an economical aspect to this as well. I asked Jerry how they could afford it, and he told me it wasn't really that bad. The tickets to local events were fairly inexpensive, and they often got discounts or free tickets. I know from experience that Jerry could always get us good prices for concert tickets. He could usually talk you into giving him a deal.

The Disney trips were another matter. Disney never gave discounts for tickets or rooms, but they could fly relatively cheaply on Jet Blue.

Jerry – "Jet Blue always treated Alex special, even allowing him to sit in the cockpit once, on our first trip. They couldn't help us enough. They were great."

As a matter of fact, everyone at the airport and airlines, including the TSA officials always took care of them.

Jerry and Penny both worked hard and sacrificed, to give Alex the things that he not only needed, but that would bring him happiness. Of course, they had to go without, like that new outfit or newer appliance or a later model car, to make a good life for Alex, but it was easy. He was the center of their world. Despite all his needs and handicaps, Alex had a full, fun life.

Chapter 19 – The 'Mayor' of Malden

City events were a big part of Alex's life. Jerry, Penny, and Alex went everywhere in the city of Malden. Jerry would look in the paper each week for events to attend. There was always something going on. Parades, picnics, fireworks, fairs, Jerry, Penny, and Alex did it all. One of Alex's biggest fans is the Mayor of Malden, Gary Christenson.

Gary came to know Alex and his parents through the Malden public school system, with which he was deeply involved.

Gary – "If we were at an event together, we would try to make sure Alex knew how much we appreciated having him in our city."

Gary is a triple alumnus of Suffolk University, with a Bachelor's degree in Political Science and Business Management (1990), a Masters Degree in Public Administration (1992), and a Juris Doctorate from Suffolk University Law School (i.e. Dr of Jurisprudence) (2003). He was elected mayor of Malden in 2011 and took office the following year.

Gary – "I dreamt of becoming mayor when I was a junior in high school."

He worked five years on the School Committee and eight years on the City Council. He's been the Mayor of Malden for the last eight years and is a lifelong Democrat.

Gary – "As mayor I wanted to get involved with the schools as much as possible. Malden High, where I went to school and graduated, was just across the street from City Hall, so I just tried to immerse myself in as many activities as possible, and that's where I got to meet Alex."

Jerry – "When we went to events at school, like plays, and games, and concerts, Gary was always there."

Jerry would talk to the teachers who ran the events afterward, and they'd say they had never worked at a place where the Mayor goes to see their productions.

Jerry – "That's what he does. It's exceptional."

Gary – "Alex was the impetus. We have been screaming out for people to take pride and Alex did."

He did that by attending the offsite school events.

Gary - "How can you not be at these events when Alex was there?"

The mayor of the city seems to have an enlightened attitude. There was always something to do in town. Gary would meet with the fire chief every two weeks and the police chief every week. They were always looking at the calendar to see what events were coming up.

Alex especially liked the parades they had in town.

Jerry – "During parades, everyone, the police, the firemen, Shriners, and strangers, would stop by and say hi to Alex, including the mayor of Malden. Everyone seemed to know him, although they were all strangers to us."

Gary Christenson wasn't the only mayor to step out of a parade to say hi to Alex.

During a New Years Eve parade at Copley Square in Boston, Alex was sitting with Penny and Jerry watching the marchers, when Marty Walsh, the Mayor of Boston, stopped and said Happy New Year to Alex.

At another parade in Boston during Veterans' Day festivities, Mayor Walsh again stepped out of the parade and said hi to Alex.

If twice wasn't enough, it happened again.

Jerry – "We went to the Fourth of July celebration at Faneuil Hall one time and the Mayor was there with U.S. Ambassador Ray Flynn, giving a speech. So we stopped and watched, and at the end of his talk, the press and everyone ran up to talk to him and ask questions. They were all crowding around him. When he noticed Alex he told everyone to stop, he had to say hi to someone. So he and Ambassador Flynn came over and took pictures with Alex and signed their autographs."

There was an article about it in the Globe. The picture, a piece of history, hangs on their hallway wall.

The city of Malden had a big impact on Alex and his family, but they also had an impact on the city.

Gary – "I learned a lot from Alex."

Alex was special in a very unique way.

Gary – "As mayor I deal with a lot of negativity, a lot of complaints, a lot of people questioning why they're here. But Alex always reminded me why things are good, to be a good person, to have pride, to care. It just reminded me of the meaning of life, which we often forget about in this crazy world we live in. Alex was someone who made you feel good about where you lived."

In his interactions with the city of Malden over his life, Alex seemed to have drawn people together. They gravitated toward him, for some reason. Maybe it was his smile.

Gary — "When you saw Alex, all your problems and what was going on went away. One of the proudest moments for me as mayor was seeing how his peers, regular kids his own age, treated him."

Friendliness, dignity, and respect, these are the attitudes and ideas Gary and Dana and others in the city's school system are trying to instill. If Alex's life was any indication, they did a good job. Malden is one of the most diverse communities in a metropolis of diversity, and as the city went, so went the public high school.

Gary — "Malden High School was recently deemed the most diverse high school in Massachusetts, number one in over 351 cities and towns, seventh in the country."

What makes this unusual is the unique mix of races - 25% Asian, 24% black, 23% Latino, and 22% white, an almost even split.

Gary — "Wherever you go, into whatever district, you find the same mix."

Malden seems to be increasingly more inclusive, while Boston schools appear to have become more segregated over the last few years.

Gary — "We are so diverse here race will never be an issue for us. As an overall district, we're in the top five of the state."

Accordingly to Gary, "You don't know who you are going to meet on any given day in Malden, the races are so evenly split."

As mayor, Gary says it is something that has been very enriching for him.

Gary — "I'm experiencing things I would never have experienced in any other city, because of the mixture of people. And everyone gets along. Back to the complaints, we hardly ever have complaints about racial issues. The shift was in the year 2000, when the word inclusion began to take hold."

From the city's perspective, it meant finding the funding and budgets to support these inclusive programs.

Gary — "At first we had to outsource many of these programs, but we knew that if we had the right amount of resources, we could keep these Special Needs children in our own system. That's an on-going challenge."

If a parent can't get the services they need within the city school system, they have to go outside it. This costs the city millions of dollars, according to Gary. If the city has the budgets, it can provide those services, experts, and facilities the people need. It can be a slow process when trying to balance all the other needs.

Gary – "When we had a major crisis with the school budget, we decided that whatever we had above the maintenance budget, anything over that had to go to Special Ed and nothing else. That's because of the impact Alex and others had over the years on the city and school system."

This has helped develop a philosophy going forward so that when constructing a budget, city and school leaders look at the Special Ed programs first, instead of it being a late addition. Special Needs are no longer an afterthought in Malden. Inclusion starts right at the beginning.

Gary would call Alex, the Mayor. "The Mayor's here," he would say, and everyone would know who he meant and scatter. That's how Alex became the honorary unofficial mayor of Malden.

Penny – "Gary is one of the most supportive people in the city."

Gary – "I always appreciated what Alex did for me and the city, and we're never going to forget it by making sure something is done in his honor that lets future generations know the positive impact he had on our city[26]."

Gary gave Alex a special citation on behalf of the city of Malden for his eighteenth birthday.

City of Malden Citation

Citation

On this day, the City of Malden wishes

Alex Gentile

A Happy 18th Birthday! Alex is a dear friend and I am proud to say one of Malden High School's most enthusiastic sports fans. Not only does he attend many of the games to cheer on the Blue and Gold but he also participates in Unified Sports and in the Challenger

---

[26] See Chapter 26 – Alex's Legacy

League. Again, we wish Alex a Happy Birthday and many more happy and healthy years ahead. Go MALDEN!

GARY CHRISTENSON, Mayor
Sunday, September 28, 2014

Mayor Gary and Me

Figure 14 - Mayor Christenson presents his citation to Alex

The city is also having the field where Alex played Challenger League baseball renamed after him.

When Alex turned eighteen, Jerry applied for legal guardianship over Alex, with Penny as his caregiver, so that they would get Adult Foster Care aid. This was a big help. They also applied for food stamps, but were turned down because Jerry did Alex's cooking and shopping. Taking care of Alex didn't get easier as he grew older, just the opposite, but Penny and Jerry made it look easy. It took planning, preparation, and sacrifice.

For a lot of people it can be difficult to bring up a child with special needs. You need a network of family and friends for support. The school system and city have to provide the needed services, which can have a profound impact on a child's life. Alex appears to have had all these things and exceptional parents, as well, a perfect storm of support. Forestdale, Special Olympics, Malden High, Challenger League, Unified Sports, all happened just as Alex came on the scene.

Chapter 20 – Trials and Tribulations

Giving Alex a full life and making him part of their every activity was not always easy, although Penny and Jerry sometimes made it seem that way. In fact, almost every day was a struggle. There were many obstacles and attitudes to be overcome. It took persistence, determination, strength, and a fierce, relentless love to succeed. That Penny and Jerry met and defeated these obstacles is a testament to them. It was heroic. They were exceptional parents.

There were constantly recurring issues, including things like no access and no changing facility.

Penny – "Some places were hard to get into and not handicap accessible."

Even a simple visit to the doctor's office, a place where they should have understood Alex's needs and condition, could be trying.

Jerry told me that they used to take Alex to his appointments at the scheduled time, but because the doctor always got backed up, they'd have to sometimes wait for hours.

"We'd have an appointment for three and end up waiting until six to see the doctor."

No one ever checked to see how they were doing or informed them of the status of their appointment. They were totally left in the dark.

Jerry - "The doctor would be mad because Alex didn't respond like he wanted him to and seemed sluggish, but he had been sitting there for three hours!"

After a few such experiences, Jerry stopped being polite and asking nicely.

"I wouldn't take no for an answer after awhile, and that would lead to arguments. I would yell and swear," he confessed. He would tell them, "I don't care how, just get it done!"

It was a never-ending battle. The same things kept occurring over and over again.

Jerry – "No matter how good people were and how hard they tried, issues always occurred. To them it was no big deal, just an isolated case, but to us it happened all the time."

Even the simplest things could be a drama. Many people, even doctors, did not understand or respect Alex's condition. Some did not have any sensibility toward him.

Once, when Alex was twelve, he had strep throat. As was mentioned earlier, Alex was unable to keep his mouth open. Any kind of dental work like a cleaning or a filling required sedating him in the OR. His dentist used a wedge or two tongue-depressor sticks when he examined him.

When they first looked at Alex in the emergency room to determine that he had strep, they had used the tongue-depressors. When Alex was admitted his parents told the doctor about this issue and she called for a dentist to help her. However, the dentist informed everyone that they no longer used a wedge for this purpose. Instead, against Jerry's wishes, he used a reverse hemostat. To make matters worse, instead of putting it in the side of Alex's mouth, as Jerry recommended, he put it in the middle. Alex bit down on it during the procedure, breaking four of his teeth at the gum line and almost fracturing his jaw.

It was a horror show, all because no one listened to Penny and Jerry.

It got worse.

The dentist proceeded to repair Alex's gum line and reset the teeth. Jerry told him they'd have to sedate Alex to work on his teeth, but the dentist said he couldn't use a sedative because he was afraid of the effect of the anesthesia, since Alex had strep throat. Instead, he wanted to give Alex a shot of morphine in his mouth. Jerry asked him how long the work would take. The doctor replied that it would take about fifteen minutes. He intended to repair the gum line and fix the fractured teeth by wiggling them back in place with his fingers while Alex was still awake, using the reverse hemostats again! Not only that, he got mad at Jerry for interfering.

So Jerry said, "OK. I'm going to grab your balls and every time Alex wrenches in pain I'm going to squeeze them."

They ended up using the anesthesia while they repaired the damage they had done to his mouth

Jerry – "After the operation the doctor came out and said he was glad they didn't try it without the anesthesia. He never would have been able to do it the other way."

Alex didn't wake up for three days!

A thing we take for granted can be a nightmare for Alex and his parents.

Long time friend, Cindy Kelloway – "Jerry made sure Alex got the best treatment. If Alex wasn't being taken care of, or was being bypassed or ignored, Jerry would speak up. He usually chose his words wisely, 'I want to talk with the manager.' "

Penny took things a little easier than Jerry, but even she could get rude if she was fighting for her child.

Cindy – "Penny came from Charlestown. She could be tough-mouthed sometimes. She went to the school once to pick up Alex. She parked in a spot that she usually did when picking him up, but someone got mad because she was blocking traffic. When they complained, Penny said, 'Tough s---! I'm picking up Alex. F off!' And that was the end of it. I think it was Alex's name more than the swearing that resolved things."

Some adults at the school didn't get Alex. They didn't understand what was going on.

Dana, the school principal – "Because they didn't go out of their way to get to know Alex, or Penny and Jerry, they didn't understand him."

Sometimes conflicts arose because people just didn't know what Alex's needs were, or what Penny and Jerry's needs were as his parents. Some complained.

Dana – "I would ask them, 'Well, have you talked to them? Have you reached out to them? Do you know who Alex is? Do you know he laughs at some of the stupid things I do?' And I think that's really important when you're in a school with kids who come with abilities like Alex and other kids."

Dana goes on to explain.

"We had big problems out back of the cafeteria with the pick up and drop off of the Special Needs kids. Their vans were causing disruptions and some had complained about the traffic tie-ups."

It didn't bother Dana, but the school committee had a plan. They wanted to reroute the Special Needs kids to swing the vans off route 60 down behind an auto shop.

Dana – "I lost my temper. I went ballistic. 'Let me get this right,' I said. 'We're going to take our most vulnerable students, students that everyone already dismisses, and make them go all the way around Route 60 and drop off their child near an auto shop with fumes and chemicals and oil. And then have their parents take them down a corridor to another corridor and then up an elevator and down another corridor and then another to get to the cafeteria where they normally go?' "

He told them no chance and ruffled a few feathers. In the end, however, they realized that it probably wasn't a good idea.

Dana – "The way we have it now the Special Needs kids are at the heart of the school, where everything's happening."

It's the busiest part of the school and the Special Needs kids are right in the middle of it, included, moving through the halls with everybody else, all together. It's not, those kids, it's all of us together, all the same. Not treated like outcasts, but treated like they belong.

Dana – "There was no chance we were going to let that happen. God forbid I'd have to tell Penny she had to drop off Alex around the corner on Route 60 by the auto shop. Good luck."

Jerry didn't expect trouble when he took Alex out. He didn't start out mad. He always looked forward to participating in the off-campus activities and showing Alex's school spirit. Unfortunately, it sometimes ended up in a verbal battle.

One evening Jerry took Alex to a basketball game. When he got there, there were thirty steps leading up to the auditorium. The attendant, a teacher, told them there was another door around the back, but that it was chained up. He then proceeded to tell Jerry that the last time this happened they had two or three guys carry the kid and his chair up the stairs. Jerry said, "You call yourself a teacher? You haven't learned anything. Why haven't you unlocked the doors? Why didn't you fix the problem?" Next time they went the rear door was unlocked so Alex could get in.

Jerry – "A lot of people aren't used to dealing with special needs."

They went to another basketball game in Everett where there was no handicapped seating and nowhere for Alex to sit. They told Jerry the only place they could go was way down at the other end of the stands, out past the court where they couldn't see anything.

Jerry said, "Why don't you just put us out in the hall?"

Instead of taking Alex all the way to the other end of the auditorium, Jerry put him right on the court and sat behind him, pushing the players and refs away when they backed into him too closely.

It didn't matter who they were. If they endangered or disrespected Alex, they would hear about it.

Jerry – "One day we went to a Feast Day Parade in the North End and the cops drove by on their motorcycles almost hitting Alex, who was standing by the side of the road."

Jerry went ballistic. He didn't care that they were cops. They had almost run over his kid. They apologized and put someone there to keep the traffic away from Alex.

However, some people and places got it.

Jerry – "At a Danvers's football game we went to, we were brought through the crowd to a perfect seat and asked repeatedly by the attendants if we wanted anything."

A little thoughtfulness can make a world of difference to a Special Needs child and their parents.

Paula, Penny's next door neighbor – "A lot of parents with Special Needs kids don't, or are unable to, take the child with them and do things with them. They took Alex everywhere. Alex participated and loved it. People they didn't know would say hi to him and take pictures with him. He had a wonderful life."

Penny and Jerry fought fiercely and constantly to ensure their child had that full, happy life.

Including and caring for the needs of a child like Alex can be challenging and seem overwhelming. You can't do it alone.

Dana (on teaching in an inclusive high school) – "You're dealing with young people between fourteen and twenty-two. If you don't love that and embrace it, don't do it, do something else, because it is hard work. It's rewarding, but it's challenging. There were days when Jerry and I were fast friends, but there were also days when he'd pass by my secretary, barge into my office, and say, 'We need to talk.' I'd say, 'OK, let's figure out what's happening.' "

Dana would usually play the role of mediator, "Let me deal with that and get that solved." He says he tried not to ever get mad or upset.

Dana – "I knew why Jerry was down there. He wasn't there for himself or Penny. He was down there for his kid and his kid had more needs than most. His kid needed something and I felt it was our job to figure out what was going awry."

Since Dana lived in the same town as Alex and his parents he had the advantage of knowing Penny and Jerry before they came to the high school. As a matter of fact, they had family connections. Penny went to the same school as Dana's wife and Jerry was friends with his brother-in-law. Dana thought this helped the situation.

Dana (laughs) – "It doesn't leave you any room to take short cuts, or dismiss them, because you have to answer to all your family and friends if Jerry or Penny didn't get what they needed. Mister Wong at Kowloon wouldn't treat me right."

Chapter 21 – Alex's Girls

Alex was lucky to have several close friends growing up, many who had been visiting and playing with him at school since the first grade, most of them girls. Three of them are the daughters of Bobbi Jo MacDonald, Penny's best friend through Alex's teenage years. It was her daughter, Skye, who introduced her to Penny and Jerry.

Skye MacDonald is twenty-three now. She first met Alex when she was in second grade at the Forestdale School in Malden.

Skye – "I was six or seven. A pre-school teacher asked if I wanted to come to her class during recess."

She was so young that she didn't know they had special needs, and just thought of them as other kids.

Skye – "There were six kids in the room and I noticed a little boy with a book in his hand."

It was Alex. She liked books so went over to talk to him.

Skye – "He didn't respond, but he smiled and listened to me, which was good, because I liked to talk."

She met Alex's parents that day.

Skye – "I volunteered to dismiss him from class and pushed his chair out and met Penny and Jerry. My mom (Bobbi Jo) was also there. They all became good friends."

Skye went to the special class every day during recess and special elective activities like arts and crafts. She did this from second grade to eighth.

Skye – "It was a lot of fun to be with them and to try and help them."

She would read books to them, walk with them or push them, and help feed them. Eventually she started hanging with Alex out of school, at birthday parties and at his house when her mom visited. She had a close relationship with Alex.

Skye – "It was Dawn, the Special Ed teacher in Alex's class at Forestdale that inspired me to become a Special Ed teacher."

Skye was not disturbed when she realized that Alex had special needs.

"Skye – "My grandfather was in an accident that left him a paraplegic and brain damaged. I saw that he was different, but I was used to seeing him, so thought nothing of it."

She was bothered by the way some people, kids and grownups, looked or acted on seeing Alex.

Skye – "They'd act weird, and pointed or stared, or whispered, as if they didn't know what to do or how to act. They were obviously uncomfortable. They missed the rewards of knowing him."

Skye would babysit and care for deaf and blind kids outside of school.

Motivated by her grade school teacher and a lifelong desire to help people, Skye has gone on to study Special Ed at Wheelock College in Boston. She works in pubic schools with emotional and behavioral disorders instead of severe disorders.

Skye – "I got into it by accident through a program for non-academic scholarships, but it was something I always wanted to do. It kind of fell into my lap.

"Emotional and behavioral work is more quick-paced than with the severely disabled like Alex. It requires a lot of patience and confidence. You must be creative and animated to keep their interest."

They also employ things like the martial arts to improve their self-esteem and self-control.

Skye was drawn to Alex because of his energy.

Skye – "He had a great personality. He was so sassy. He would stick his tongue at me and make noises. He was really interactive. He especially liked to be tickled. He would lift up his shirt and invite you to tickle him. He was the clown of the class, a funny jokester."

Skye feels she and Alex found each other by fate, that it was meant to be.

"Alex changed my life and taught me a lot about people. He inspired me to be an advocate for Special Needs children. He affected everyone who met him."

Another friend of Alex was Skye's younger sister, Aryzona. Aryzona is twenty-one, the same age as Alex. They were in the same grade through elementary school and high school, although in a different class. They were at the prom together, although not with each other. You cannot hear a story about Alex without Aryzona's name being mentioned.

She, like her sister, used to visit the Special Needs classroom during recesses and lunch times.

Aryzona MacDonald – "I've known Alex all my life, through my mom, who was Alex's mother's best friend. I would visit his class during recess when at Kindergarten. Alex always had a smile. He was a genuinely happy kid."

They would play like typical kids. She didn't know Alex was different until she started walking him to the cafeteria when they were in the sixth grade.

Aryzona – "In 6th and 7th grades I would walk with Alex to the cafeteria. I was struck by how people treated Alex differently than a normal kid, and began to realize that he was special. In high school they were much more inclusive and accepting of his differences."

In 7th and 8th grades Aryzona would visit Alex's class for a whole period and help the teachers, but she doesn't remember how or why this occurred. Naturally they would play together when their mothers, who were best friends, visited each other.

Aryzona remembers when Alex would come to her volleyball games with his parents. She liked the fact that Penny and Jerry were there to watch her play, because her mother worked and usually didn't come to the games.

Aryzona goes to Centre College in Kentucky and is majoring in Psychology. She likes to study and know why people do the things they do, so she can help them. She eventually wants to be a nurse.

"I always wanted to help people," she told me.

She went to the college because of a Leadership and Merit Scholarship she won in high school, working in student government and fundraising activities.

Aryzona – "It was sometimes a challenge to make Alex smile, but it was worth it when he did."

As if Skye and Aryzona weren't enough, there's one more MacDonald we need to hear from, sixteen-year-old Shawna.

Shawna is currently a junior in High School, who likes math and history, but isn't a big fan of science, especially chemistry.

Like her sisters, Shawna also visited Alex when she was young, and thinks his teacher at the time, Dawn, taught him a lot.

Shawna knew Alex for as long as she can remember. Penny called her mom, Bobbi Jo, Auntie B.

Shawna – "They used to come and visit my mom and I would play with him. He liked to be tickled. We were always around each other at one house or the other."

Their relationship continued into high school, in Unified Sports, where her gym class would work together with the Special Needs class.

Shawna — "Alex would come to all our volleyball and softball games. He was the team's number one fan."

The girls and their mom are all part of Team Alex.

"We had all the T-shirts, one for each year," says Shawna.

She told me that she learned a lot about Special Needs kids from Alex, and wants to help people because of him.

Shawna — "I could always get him to smile. I loved his smile."

Besides Bobby Jo's girls, there are two other lifelong friends of Alex who deserve special mention, Samantha French and Alyssa Figueiredo.

Samantha French (Sam) — "I met Alex through a friend of my parents, through Bobbi Jo, Skye, and Aryzona. I've known him all my life."

The first time she met him she was immediately struck by his smile. It's the first thing she remembers about him.

Sam - "He had the most amazing smile."

Samantha and Alex were in school together from the 4th grade until they graduated from high school. Like her friends, Skye and Aryzona, she would visit the Special Needs classroom every day during recess and lunch.

Sam — "Aryzona and I and another girl named Megan Doherty would spend lunch in the Special Needs class playing with Alex."

She did it on her own and found it very rewarding.

Sam - "He kept us on our toes, pulling him around, trying to make him smile. We were his girlfriends. He was a player."

They often fought for his attention.

Sam — "We are better for being around him. He gave off great vibes. He made you feel good."

They also played with the other Special Needs kids in Alex's class, one of whom was a boy in a wheelchair named James.

Sam — "He was Alex's best friend and could communicate and understand a little."

Samantha told me that none of the other kids in her class ever commented on what she was doing, but when they'd question her about it, she'd say, "It's fun. You should go."

Sam was very close to Penny and Jerry, who are like second parents to her. She admires how they took care of Alex, how much they loved him and showed their love. It was one of the reasons she spent so much time with him.

When I commented on how lucky Alex was to have such friends, she responded by telling me they were the lucky ones for knowing Alex.

Samantha confirms everything Gary and Dana say about Jerry and Alex.

Sam — "In High School I was in the Play Production Program (drama class). We did about three plays a year. Alex and Jerry came to every one, sometimes more than once. They came to all of our volleyball and softball games, even some of the away games. Alex would stick to Jerry and was the center of attention. Everyone knew him and came over to say hi. Alex would watch the game. His attention was on the field or stage. He followed Jerry's lead when to cheer."

Like his other girlfriends, Sam attended the Senior Prom with Alex[27]. He had the seat of honor. There's a picture of him sitting there with all the girls around him. He danced with all of them.

Sam — "We made him dance with all of us, even when he didn't want to."

They would support him as they danced.

---

[27] He went with Annabelle Krupcheck – see Chapter 22.

Figure 15 - Alex at the prom with his girlfriends, from left to right, Taylor Figueiredo, Samantha French, Alyssa Figueiredo, Shannon Gibson, Alex Gentile, Jillian Powers, Meghan Doherty, Samantha Kiernan, Samantha Dorazio

Sam – "Alex was sassy. He'd look away when you came over and then peek at you shyly. He would make you work for it to make him laugh. He knew you really wanted to make him laugh."

She saw his progress over time.

Sam – "They told his parents he would never walk, but they were determined and he finally learned to walk. You'd see him walking down the hall to the cafe with his walker or with someone."

As was mentioned earlier, the Special Needs kids had their own classrooms, but in the spirit of inclusiveness, they would mix with the regular students in the cafeteria. The SN kids all sat together, since they needed assistance.

Sam – "The other kids would always stop and say hi to Alex."

She never felt bad or sorry for Alex.

Sam – "He was having too much fun. How can you feel sorry for someone that is having the best time, going to Disney once a year and to baseball games at Fenway. What a great life Penny and Jerry gave him. He was the star of the show."

Samantha joined the Navy Reserves on graduating from High School, and went to boot camp and naval school. She's currently going to Salem State, majoring in nursing. She's a people person, who always wanted to work with people.

Sam – "I like helping people."

Alex helped her in return.

Sam – "In Naval boot camp they have what they call Battle Stations, which is our graduation test. It's really hard, and my friends were there holding motivational signs. Alex was there with a sign, too. It really helped me get through it. If Alex can do it and overcome his difficulties, so can I."

Now she's in the reserves and has to go to Newport, RI, one weekend per month and two weeks a year. She was always the go-to person when someone was having problems. She liked making a difference in people's lives. Now with her naval training and experience, she'll be able to do even more.

When I commented how she surely made a difference in Alex's life, she told me that Alex made a difference in hers.

Samantha has lived in Malden all her life and loved going to Malden High.

Sam – "I loved the teachers. They were very involved. I always felt safe, comfortable, and happy there. It's the most diverse school in a very diverse city, with a real mix of races."

She loved the diversity and that everyone got along. She also thought Dana was the best principal she ever saw.

Sam – "He knew everyone by name, and was very involved He always took interest in what students were doing, whether it was a big deal or small."

No one person inspired her. It was more the community, the team of people around her supporting her and each other. Support was everywhere, especially from the teachers.

Sam – "My drama teacher, Sean Walsh, was good. I learned about myself in his class. There were all sorts of kids there, jocks, geeks. I learned you have to be yourself no matter what anybody says."

Samantha cannot say enough about Penny and Jerry.

Sam – "They never denied him or restricted him, never felt bad for themselves. They were proud of Alex and loved to bring him around. Alex inspired many people. He worked hard and learned to do many things people thought he couldn't do. He was an awesome 'feel good' person."

Alex's death came as a shock. She knew he had been in the hospital with seizures, but wasn't expecting him not to come home one day. She was speechless when her mother told her. They went to the hospital that morning.

Sam — "It was just devastating. I took him for granted and always thought he'd be around."

Alyssa Figueiredo is another lifelong friend of Alex's.

Alyssa — "I don't remember when I first met Alex. I've known him all my life."

She went to elementary school and high school with him, along with Aryzona and Samantha, all who were in the same grade.

Alyssa — "I would go down to the Special Needs classroom(s) during lunch and recess with the other girls. I was part of the group. That's what we did."

She heard them talking about it and decided to go, too.

Alyssa has a younger cousin with special needs, so is used to someone with disabilities and not uncomfortable. She was part of Team Alex with her friends to cheer Alex on in the Special Olympics during middle school.

At first she thought of Alex as just one of the kids, who was fun to play with. Over the years she started getting closer to him as their families would interact, going to each others birthday parties, visiting his house and playing with him, watching videos and DVDs with him.

Alyssa — "I loved to tickle him and make him laugh."

In High School, as a freshman, she started thinking seriously about becoming a Special Ed teacher, and asked if she could get credit for a class period working with Special Needs students. The school wasn't sure at first, but eventually came up with the Peer Tutoring class, where Alyssa was able to work with the kids a couple of periods (2 classes) weekly in their classroom for credit. Alex and his friends were there. Rachel, Alex's teacher, helped. They took the kids on field trips, to the movies. Alyssa also volunteered to work with the higher-function class, as well.

As mentioned earlier, Alyssa also took part in the Unified Sports program during gym class., and played cards with him.

Alyssa — "I showed him a card with his mother and father's picture. He would smile. I was trying to get him to recognize his Mommy and Daddy."

The second class had kids with Down syndrome, cerebral palsy, autism, and emotional issues, but there was something about Alex that made him different and easier to get close to.

Alyssa was also one of the girls at the senior prom with Alex. She even remembers dancing with him in 8th grade.

Alyssa – "The fact that he was non-verbal made him different. He had a great personality. He was always happy, always smiling and laughing. He was a pretty happy kid."

Like Alex's other friends, she also learned a lot from him.

Alyssa – "He taught us how to have a good time. He reminded us how to smile. If Alex could be happy and smile, so should I."

Alyssa graduated from Malden High School in 2015, along with Alex and Aryzona. She then went to Framingham State University majoring in psychology and elementary education. Currently a senior, she's applying to graduate schools for a Special Ed degree, like Rachael, for both severe and moderate needs.

Alyssa – "They are just people like the rest of us. They have challenges just like the rest of us, but these don't define them or us. I want to give them the ability to do the things they want to do and have a full life."

In a way, Alyssa, who wanted to be a teacher since second grade, was inspired by Alex's teacher, Rachel.

Alyssa – "Like the life I saw Rachel give Alex."

Like several of the girls above, Alyssa wants to make a difference in a child's life and likes working with them.

Alyssa – "Getting them to smile is the greatest thing you can do."

It's a two way street.

Alyssa – "The kids taught me something. I learned something new every day, like how to have a good day, how to smile and enjoy life, how to be appreciative of what you have."

Alyssa has a double bond with Alex through his parents.

Alyssa – "Penny and Jerry are like my 2nd parents. They're the most incredible parents you could have. They gave Alex everything. They gave him a normal life. They did a lot of things with him. They treated him special."

A big influence on Alyssa's life was her second grade teacher, Colleen Swan, who she's still friends with. Alyssa did an internship with her in high school, where Colleen mentored her and taught her how to be a good teacher.

Alyssa — "When I was in second grade with her, Colleen said I'd be a good teacher; that I was a natural, born to work with kids."

She also told her to always follow her heart.

Alyssa — "Money is not as important as being able to work with children and make a positive difference in their lives."

Alyssa and her friends, Skye, Aryzona, Shawna, and Samantha surely made a difference in Alex's life.

Chapter 22 – Prom-Misses

A highpoint in Alex's high school experience was going to the senior prom. It was 2015, the theme, 'A Midnight in Paris'. It was held at the Danversport Yacht Club. How Alex and his date got there is a long story.

John and Sheila Krupcheck have known Penny and Jerry for seventeen years. Sheila and Penny scrapbook together, and John is related to Penny's brother Joe's wife.

Sheila (laughs) – "The first picture I saw of Alex was taken in front of the Public Gardens, and I thought it was taken at their house. I was very impressed. Then I realized they didn't have a garden. I was very surprised."

Two of John and Sheila's children are close to Alex in age. Annabelle, who is twenty-two, is the oldest, and four months order than Alex, while Nicholas (Nicky), their only boy, is twenty, one year younger than Alex. Genevieve, the youngest, is seventeen.

Sheila remembers, around 2007, she went with her kids to watch Alex, while Penny was in the Hospital with a hysterectomy. The kids were all playing together and Nicky told a joke about Santa Claus farting.

Sheila – "Well, Alex broke out laughing. He laughed out loud every time Nicky said, farting. It made Alex belly laugh. It was so funny."

The kids hung out a lot, on each and every birthday of all four of them. They thought Alex was a fun kid to be around, unaware he was Special Needs.

Sheila believes Alex knew more than many people gave him credit for. If you just listened to him you knew what he wanted.

Once when she was watching Alex, they had limited his juice intake. Alex crawled into the kitchen with his cup and shook it at Sheila. When she didn't get him more, he went to the drawer where the juice was kept and opened it. Sheila said, 'No', a word Alex understood and had heard many times before, but he ignored it and shook the cup again.

Sheila – "He kept shaking the cup and finally got the juice."

Alex would pick up and hand you the box of the video he wanted to watch.

Sheila — "I felt like Alex was my nephew. The kids thought of him as their cousin."

They were part of Team Alex, rooting for him in the Special Olympics each summer. All their kids would go and cheer in their T-shirts.

Penny and Sheila spent a lot of time together, going to scrapbook parties and family events with Penny's brother Joe and her sister-in-law, Kim, all the birthday parties, babysitting, and so on. They were family. John sponsored Alex at his confirmation. The kids didn't think of him as a Special Needs kid. They thought his smile lit up the room.

Actually, they had a lot in common with Alex. Their family went to Disney World often. The kids loved Penny and Jerry.

Sheila's daughter, Annabelle, was one grade ahead of Alex, and graduated from Danvers High in 2014. She was a freshman at Pace University in New York City during Alex's senior year.

That year Penny wanted Alex to go to the senior prom.

Jerry — "Penny and I made an appointment with the house principal, Mister Mastrangelo, to tell him we wanted to go to the prom with Alex. He told us that parents don't go to the prom. It had never been done before. I told him, 'We'll set a precedent' and he said, 'No, you can't do that.'"

They were surprised to hear this had never been done before. They thought it only natural to want to share this special time in their child's life with him. Jerry explained that most of these kids will graduate and get married, or go on to college and careers, but Alex doesn't have anything like that to look forward to, just the prom and his graduation. They wanted to be there for him. The principal said, "OK, when you put it like that, you can go."

Penny and Jerry were able to share that evening with their son, but they had to stand up for that right.

Penny — "I asked Sheila if her Annabelle would go with Alex. She called her daughter at school, who said yes immediately. Alex got to go to the prom with a college girl!"

Sheila — "I made her prom dress."

When I asked why Annabelle would take time from school and come all the way back to Massachusetts for Alex's prom, she told me that Annabelle loved Penny and Jerry, and thought of them as her 2nd parents.

Sheila — "She would do anything for them. All the kids felt this way."

Alex picked her up in a hired limo, a white Rolls Royce. He had his tux on and a corsage for her. They went to the park before the prom to take pictures. All the kids from the school were there and yelled his name when they saw him. They all came over to say hi and take pictures with him. He was the center of attention again, and danced with all his girlfriends. It made Alex smile.

Figure 16 - Annabelle and Alex at the park on way to the prom

John – "Alex made you not take things, life, for granted. Every second of Penny and Jerry's life was dedicated to Alex."

John and Sheila, and their family gravitated to Penny, Jerry, and Alex because of the joy in their family.

John – "They are the most giving people we know. They defied all the negatives and naysayers and fought for him fiercely, totally."

John observed that Alex did many things people said he would never do - survive the first days of his life, walk, keep his teeth[28]!

John – "Alex thrived and lived as long as he did because of Penny and Jerry, who made sure he enjoyed life to the fullest."

It was a life full of love.

Annabelle is working toward her masters of Fine Arts in New Media at New Jersey University. She's a sketch artist, and recently published a book of poems with her own pictures. She drew a picture of Alex and Minnie Mouse, which hangs in the hallway, right across from Alex's room. It's far better than the Disney one.

Their son, Nicky, is a sophomore at Gettysburg College, majoring in Japanese and Religious Studies. Genevieve, who was probably the closest to Alex of all their kids, is a senior at Danvers High and wants to be a publisher.

When Genevieve was three or four, during the birthday parties, she would crawl away to find a nice quiet spot to sit alone. Alex would crawl over and sit with her. They would watch all the same videos.

Sheila – "They were good, sweet, generous kids with Alex. They really loved him, and are like that with everyone now."

Alex helped teach them how to be that way.

John – "Everyone who knew Alex got more from him than he got from them. Our lives were enriched by knowing him."

Sheila – "Our kids learned love, empathy, and compassion through knowing Alex. They benefited from being around him."

Part of Alex is still with them, and will be throughout their lives.

---

[28] They typically remove the teeth of kids like Alex because it's easier in the long run, but Jerry wouldn't let them.

Chapter 23 – Alex and the Church

Alex's parents were not only concerned with his physical and emotional well-being, filling his life with joy and activity, they were also concerned with his spiritual well-being, his soul. In their attempts to give him a full and meaningful life, they wanted him to partake of all the things a typical child with religious parents would do. Jerry and Penny were Roman Catholics and Penny wanted Alex to have the Eucharist. He had already been christened (baptized). Now they wanted him to have his first communion and become part of the church.

In 2004, when Alex turned seven, Penny and Jerry began going to mass at a local Catholic church, so that Alex could have his first communion. When Penny called the parish to talk to the priest and explain their situation, that Alex was a special needs child and non-verbal, she received a shock. The priest said he wouldn't allow it. He told her that because Alex couldn't understand the basic tenets of faith and didn't have the spiritual understanding required for first communion, he couldn't do it. All this without ever meeting them!

She was mortified and saddened, but if we know anything by now about Penny and Jerry, we know they would not sit still and take no for an answer, not where Alex was concerned. They had heard the word, no, many times before and like Alex, it didn't stop them.

They went to a second church, St. Joseph in Malden, and talked to Father Bill Minnegan, who happily allowed it.

Jerry took Alex to mass every Sunday for the next ten years until after his confirmation in April, 2013.

Jerry – "Sometimes Alex would make noise during mass and I would go to leave, but Father Bill would say 'Don't go', and we'd stay."

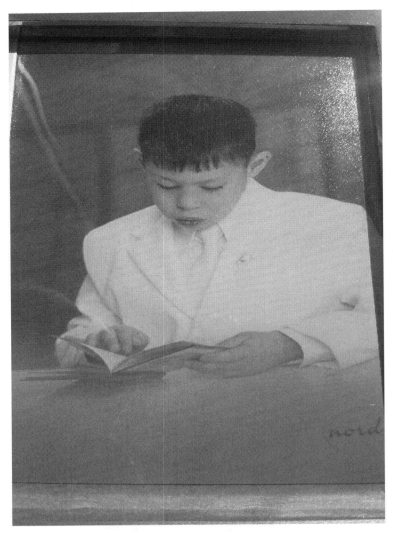

Figure 17 - Alex at his First Communion

They stopped going a few years before Alex passed away, but Alex was part of the church and got his sacraments. Even more important, Alex enjoyed it. He was around people and ceremony and music. He was part of it. He was blessed in many ways and gave back by being there.

Still, there were some who would have denied Alex the right to partake fully in the sacraments of the Catholic Church. It is a complex and potentially controversial subject, and many have given it much thought through the ages. For Alex and his family, it was real and emotional. Even within the church itself, this question continues to confront us.

The Catholic Church insists it is committed to affirming the dignity of every human being, and wants to grow in its understanding of the gifts and needs of those who live with disabilities. They want to encourage their participation in the sacraments. In this regard, it has issued guidelines for celebrating the sacraments with Special Needs persons.

The United States Conference of Catholic Bishops[29] states that it is essential that all forms of the liturgy be completely accessible to persons with disabilities and that to exclude members of the parish from these celebrations of the life of the Church, even by passive omission, is to deny the reality of that community. Accessibility involves far more than physical alterations to parish buildings. Realistic provision must be made for Catholics with disabilities to participate fully in the Eucharist and other liturgical celebrations.

This being the case, it is surprising to learn that at least one catholic priest thought to deny Alex and his parents that right. The preface to the Conference's guidelines admits that pastoral practice with regard to the sacraments varies greatly from diocese to diocese, even from parish to parish.

Inconsistencies arise for many reasons, from physical provision for accessibility, to the availability of catechetical programs for persons with intellectual, developmental, and other disabilities, also because of misunderstandings about the nature of disabilities and uncertainty about the appropriate application of church law toward persons with special needs. Fear and unfamiliarity also lead to inconsistencies.

The guideline developed by the Conference of Catholic Bishops was meant to address many of these concerns and forge a greater consistency in the practice of the sacraments. The guidelines draw upon the Church's ritual books, its canonical tradition, and its experience with persons with disabilities, in order to dispel misunderstandings.

---

[29] See usccb.org - United States Conference of Catholic Bishops Guidelines for the Celebration of the Sacraments with Persons with Disabilities

Its authors present the guidelines as a set of general principles to provide access to the sacraments for persons with disabilities. As a set of general or guiding principles, the guidelines state the following:

1. All human beings are equal in dignity in the sight of God. Moreover, by reason of their baptism, all Catholics also share the same divine calling.

2. Catholics with disabilities have a right to participate in the sacraments as fully as other members of the local ecclesial community. "Sacred ministers cannot deny the sacraments to those who seek them at appropriate times, are properly disposed, and are not prohibited by law from receiving them."

3. Parish sacramental celebrations should be accessible to persons with disabilities and open to their full, active, and conscious participation, according to their capacity. Pastoral ministers should not presume to know the needs of persons with disabilities, but should rather—before all else—consult with them or their advocates before making determinations about the accessibility of a parish's facilities and the availability of its programs, policies, and ministries. Full accessibility should be the goal for every parish, and these adaptations are to be an ordinary part of the liturgical life of the parish.

It goes on to state that the goal should be to welcome and seek out those with disabilities, and encourage participation, and so on, regarding access and services. Finally, they recognize that difficult situations may be encountered by those making pastoral decisions, and they are encouraged to establish appropriate policies for handling such instances, which respect the rights of all involved, and which ensure the necessary provision of evaluation and recourse. But things get sticky when it comes to Holy Communion, the sacrament of the Eucharist, which is central to the church.

The Eucharist is called the 'most august sacrament' in the Church, the summit and the source, the center of all Christian worship and life. And this has led to some compelling issues, such as Alex being denied participation in that sacrament.

Parents or guardians, together with pastors, are urged to see to it that children who have reached the use of reason are correctly prepared as early as possible. Pastors are to be vigilant lest any children come to the 'Holy Banquet' who have not reached the use of reason or whom they judge are not sufficiently disposed. It is important to note, however, that the criterion for reception of Holy Communion is the same for persons with intellectual and developmental disabilities as for all persons, namely, that the person be able to "distinguish the body of Christ from ordinary food," even if this recognition is evidenced through manner, gesture, or reverential silence rather than verbally.

Pastors are encouraged to 'consult with parents, those who take the place of parents, diocesan personnel involved with disability issues, psychologists, religious educators, and other experts in making their judgment'. (The priest who made the decision to deny Alex Communion (over the phone) appears to have done none of this, nor consulted with anyone else.) If it is determined that a parishioner who is disabled is not ready to receive the sacrament, "great care is to be taken in explaining the reasons for this decision. Cases of doubt should be resolved in favor of the right of the Catholic to receive the sacrament. The existence of a disability is not considered in and of itself as disqualifying a person from receiving Holy Communion."

It goes on to state that in many instances, simple accommodations can be very helpful, and should be embraced by all at the parish level. Those with special needs like feeding tubes, and other issues like Alzheimers, will also need special consideration, which are all covered in the Bishops' guidelines.

The case [30] where a Catholic church in Floresville, Texas turned away an eight-year-old boy from his First Communion because he had cerebral palsy caused a lot of controversy and got nationwide news coverage. The priest insisted that the boy had "the mental capacity of a six-month old" and didn't have "sufficient knowledge of Christ" to participate in the religious rite, even though Catholic doctrine doesn't specify what level of intelligence is adequate. The boy's family cried "discrimination", and said the priest's decision had shaken their faith. "I hurt for my grandson and my family," said the grandmother.

A deacon from the Archdiocese of San Antonio told ABC News.com that the decision whether to give the sacrament lies with the local priest, but emphasized, "It's never our desire, hope, or wish to withhold a sacrament from someone who wants or needs it."

Because there is a plurality of Christian accounts of the Eucharist, there is a plurality of practices and traditions concerning the norms for participation of those who have an intellectual disability[31]. Some Christian traditions maintain that a theological understanding of the sacrament is necessary to receive the Eucharist, some maintain that

[30] See abcnews.go.com – Article by Susan Donaldson James.
[31] See wikipedia.org - Communion and the Developmentally Disabled.

spiritual devotion to the real presence of Jesus Christ is necessary, still other traditions understand the practice of Eucharist principally as a communal expression. However, the fact is that many contemporary Christian traditions and communities do not administer the sacrament of Eucharist to intellectually disabled and/or mentally ill persons.

Thomas Aquinas maintained that all cognitively impaired Christians have a right to the Eucharist and that the sacrament should not be withheld from such persons, except in the most extreme of circumstances. According to Aquinas, the extreme circumstance that warrants withholding the Eucharist from a cognitively impaired Christian is if the Christian is entirely incapable of expressing their desire to receive the Eucharist. The worry of Aquinas was that the Eucharist would be forced upon someone who did not want to participate in the sacrament.

The rationale is developed on the understanding that persons who lack the use of reason, like infants, need the assistance of others to participate in the sacraments of the Church. Thus, ecclesial care for infants provides the principles for the ecclesial care of intellectually disabled persons. Church law states the following regarding the administration of Eucharist to children and other persons who lack the use of reason:

> "§1. The administration of the Most Holy Eucharist to children requires that they have sufficient knowledge and careful preparation so that they understand the mystery of Christ according to their capacity and are able to receive the body of Christ with faith and devotion."

> "§2. The Most Holy Eucharist, however, can be administered to children in danger of death if they can distinguish the body of Christ from ordinary food and receive communion reverently."

This policy is reflected in the positions published by many Roman Catholic dioceses in the United States and was obviously used by the priest who denied Alex and his family the sacrament.

But further reading indicates that children who are mentally retarded are to be admitted to the Eucharist when they express a desire for the sacrament and in some way manifest their reverence for it. In cases of profound retardation, "the Eucharist may be shared without further requirements, as long as the child is able to consume the sacred elements."

So it seems like it depends on the particular priest whether a particular Special Needs child can partake in the sacrament of Holy

128

Communion. Jerry and Penny were savvy enough to go to another church, and lucky enough to find a pastor who was willing to meet their needs. But maybe we should let the Pope himself have the last word on this subject[32].

As part of the Holy Year of Mercy, Pope Francis called for the disabled to have access to the sacraments, and condemned those who want to "eliminate" them, meaning in part, terminating children diagnosed with various disabilities.

"We are familiar with the objections raised, especially nowadays, to a life characterized by serious physical limitations," Francis said as he celebrated a special Mass in Rome's St. Peter's Square.

"It's thought that sick or disabled persons cannot be happy, since they cannot live the lifestyle held up by the culture of pleasure and entertainment," he continued.

The pope complained there are those who believe anything imperfect – speaking specifically of people with disabilities – should be "kept apart, in some 'enclosure'," so they don't hold back the pace "of a false well-being."

"In some cases, we are even told that it is better to eliminate them as soon as possible, because they become an unacceptable economic burden in time of crisis," he said. "Yet what an illusion it is when people today shut their eyes in the face of sickness and disability! They fail to understand the real meaning of life, which also has to do with accepting suffering and limitations."

Pope Francis's words come as pro-life advocates warn that people with Down syndrome might disappear in the next several generations because in some places where abortion is legal, up to ninety percent of unborn children diagnosed with the condition are terminated.

"The way we experience illness and disability is an index of the love we are ready to offer," the Pope insists.

According to the Pope, the "happiness that everyone desires" can only be expressed and attained "if we are capable of loving."

When asked by a young woman named Serena, who's in a wheelchair, why some disabled people aren't able to receive communion or go to mass, the Pope said, "She puts me in a tough spot!"

"Serena spoke about one of the ugliest things among us: discrimination," he observed. "It's a terrible thing."

---

[32] See cruxnow.com/vatican/2016/06/12.

The pontiff then said that those priests and parishes that refuse to give catechesis to the disabled - deaf people and those with Down syndrome - are called "to conversion."

"It's true that to receive Communion you have to be prepared," Francis relented. "But if for instance you're deaf, you must have the possibility in that parish to prepare through sign language."

The pope then said that everyone has the same ability to grow and understand Christian doctrine, even if the learning processes are different.

"Diversity doesn't mean that those who have the five senses are better than those who are deaf, we all have the possibility of loving God," he confirmed.

Talking to the priests, Francis said that those who don't welcome everyone might as well close the door of their parishes: "Everyone or no one!"

The pope added that some might argue not everyone, such as the mentally disabled, "understands sufficiently," to which the pope replied "It's you [who say this] who doesn't understand!"

Chapter 24 – 'Scrapping'

Penny has been recording all of Alex's activities, from his first year to his last, in scrapbooks full of pictures.

Paula, Penny's neighbor – "I did photography and did a photo shoot for Alex. Penny kept after me to 'Come over and scrapbook. Come over and scrapbook'. I'm a terrible procrastinator, but Penny gave me motivation, let's put it like that."

They became very good friends who share the same hobby. It's also how Penny met another best friend, Sheila Krupcheck.

"I knew Penny through her brother Joey's wife, Kim, who is my husband's sister. We'd meet casually at family gatherings."

Sheila and her husband, John, live in Danvers with their three children. Like Penny's next door neighbor, Paula, Sheila became friends with Penny through 'scrapping'.

Shiela – "We were at a Creative Memory party that Kim held, around 2001. I was selling the material for making scrapbooks. Penny really liked it and we'd hookup to do scrapping, showing each other pictures and how to display them."

They've been close friends ever since[33].

Alex's whole life, from the day he was born to the last year of his life, is in these scrapbooks. They are a treasure-trove of memories and could form a book in themselves. It's obvious upon viewing them that they are the result of a lot of work, dedication, and above all, love. They tell the story of his life as words could never do.

The scrapbooks themselves are quite attractive, big photo-albums, with thick, stylish covers. For instance, the first book in the series, for the year 1996, has a fine-grained, dark-green, hard-bound cover with gold trimming. In this book we find Alex's baby pictures, beginning with him in an incubator at the Children's Hospital the day after he was born.

There are pictures from Alex's baptism, wearing the same christening gown Jerry wore when he was baptized, and pictures of Penny's brother, Jimmy, and sister, Marlene, holding Alex. There is also a beautiful picture of Penny and Jerry holding their new baby boy, and

---

[33] John and Sheila's daughter, Annabelle, was Alex's date for the prom (see Chapter 22).

pictures of the baptismal ceremony in the church. It doesn't take many shots to show two things. Alex is a real cute kid, and Alex has a great smile.

Each page of the books has a different backing with text and cutouts. In the first book, each page had a different theme – Sleepy Time, with Alex sleeping, Peek-a-Boo Time, with Alex looking up from under a blanket or peeking out from under a chair, Splash Time, with Alex in his basinet or plastic tub. He had long, dark hair and long eyelashes.

In this same scrap book, there are two pages of Pooh pictures, one for each month of the year, with Alex and his big Pooh Bear that Jerry bought him. The theme was 'Watch Me Grow". In the beginning Pooh Bear dwarfs Alex. By the end he's almost as big as the large stuffed animal.

Fall theme pages have Alex falling in the leaves and sitting in the pumpkin patch or on a tractor. There are also pictures of Alex's first birthday party. The Winter/Christmas theme pages show Alex in his snow suit (all you can see is his little face sticking out), and sitting on Santa's lap for the first time (he would see this same Santa every year for the next ten years). There are pictures that first Christmas of Jerry's mom holding Alex and Penny's parents holding Alex, and pictures of Alex's first New Year wearing a big felt hat.

The second scrapbook had more baby pictures of Alex from age one to about three. One theme, Play Time, has Alex sitting on the swings with Penny at the park in York, Maine, smiling, and a few 'too cute' pictures of Alex at Jerry's work sitting at his desk. Another cute one has Alex at the beach, sitting in a lawn chair.

Each page has die-cuts, little paper cutouts. The last one had cutouts of a beach with sand and water in the background. Some pictures are framed, like the ones of Alex getting his first haircut at Vincent's, where he's sitting in a carousel seat. Another has him at Ironstone farm, riding a pony. This book also has great pictures of Alex's first day of school, in September 1999, when he was three years old.

There are pages of pictures of 'Mommy and Me' with Penny and Alex, and 'Daddy and Me' on a hayride and at the Public Gardens, 'Grammy and Me' and 'Nana and Papa and Me'. All of these pages have Halloween and birthdays pictures (his 2nd). There's a funny Easter shot of Alex with sunglasses in a bunny suit, and one with Alex surrounded by all his presents and wrappings.

Another book showed Alex at all the beaches he had gone to by his tenth year. They include Myrtle Beach in South Carolina, York Beach in Maine, Devereaux in Marblehead, MA, Craigsville in Barnstable on Cape Cod, Wingersheek in Gloucester, and Sandy Beach in New Hampshire. There are pictures with Alex sitting on his lawn chair and in the sand, in the water and at the boat dock. Some of the beaches, like Myrtle and Craigsville, had beach wheelchairs, with big balloon tires.

These pictures attest to what a full and enjoyable life Alex had, and how much fun the family had together.

There are two 'Daddy and Me' books with just Jerry and Alex. The first one is quite ingenious, and shows Jerry and Alex side-by-side in matching baby pictures. It's uncanny how much they look alike.

There's Alex and Jerry in their cribs (at the same age) sleeping, both in the same position with their arms over their heads, and a picture of them on the swings. There's another of Jerry's and Alex's christening, both in the same gown (Alex, fifty years later). They look just alike, with the parents in the same position. This wasn't planned. It just turned out that way, amazingly.

In the pictures of Alex and Jerry crawling on the rug toward the camera, it's only the fact that one's in color and one's in black and white that allows them to be distinguished. One pair of matching pictures shows them both at the same age (fifty years apart) rocking on the same rocking-horse chair that Jerry's father made for him!

The second 'Daddy and Me' book was a Christmas gift from Penny to Jerry in 2005. It has a great close-up shot of Alex kissing Jerry, and pictures of them driving in the car and dressed up for Halloween. It has a nice series of nine pictures, showing Alex dressed up each year for Halloween, as Pooh (1), Tigger (2), Little Devil (3), Elmo (4), Superman (5), Clifford the big red dog (6), Sponge Bob (7), and Mickey Mouse (8 and 9). Alex gets cuter every year.

This book also has picture of Alex with his dad at Disney with the characters, and at a Red Sox game, with clever cloth die-cuts of baseball gloves and uniforms. There're several pictures of Jerry and Alex planting flowers, and at his first communion (the one he almost wasn't allowed to have), dressed in a white suit. And the beat goes on.

There's Alex with Jerry at his third birthday party in the middle of a crowd of kids, blowing out candles, and one of them at a parade and on a merry-go-round. Another one has him all dressed up in his tux, with Jerry carrying him down the aisle at Penny's brother, Joey's, wedding. There's a great one of Jerry and Alex sleeping together in the leather chair. Cherished, loving pictures.

Another book, entitled Mommy and Pooh (Penny's name for Alex), has several pictures of Penny holding Alex when he was a baby, one of her favorite things to do, also some of her watching him sleep in his crib. There are photos of them playing together at the park where Alex is blowing bubbles, and at Santa's village in New Hampshire. There are pictures of 'Pooh' kissing his mommy, and trick-or-treating together, and together at Sesame Place, in Langhorne, Pennsylvania. Wonderful memories!

There is a Halloween book showing Alex ages one through fifteen, celebrating his favorite holiday, including a great one of Alex at Forestdale School with all his friends, including Bobby Jo's daughters, Skye, Aryzona, and Shawna (see Chapter 21). There's Alex at Disney with the Seven Dwarfs and with Penny and Jerry's friends, David Bugden and his wife Lisa, who often met them at the park, and one of Penny, Jerry, and Alex in front of Cinderella's Castle on Halloween. There's a great shot of Jerry dressed like Captain Hook (he really looks like a pirate) with Alex (also in costume), and one of Alex helping Jerry carve pumpkins. What a blast they had!

Another interesting scrapbook Penny created was a Calendar Book for the year 2004. This book alternates a full-page calendar (one for each month of the year) recording all the things Alex did that month, with pictures of the activities themselves.

March shows Alex on the first day after the ramp to the house was completed[34]. April has him at the park with Bobby Jo and her daughters eating jelly beans.

June has Alex playing baseball with the Cal Ripken League[35] in Everett, and at the Public Gardens, where he went on the Swan Boats. They also visited Nubble Lighthouse in York, Maine that month.

In July Alex and his parents were at a hot air balloon festival, where Penny went up in a balloon. They were also at a carnival in Henniker, NH that month, and at an event at Glendale Park in Everett, where the wrestlers posed with Alex.

---

[34] Penny – "Installing the ramp was my friend, Bobby Jo's idea. She thought it would make things easier for Alex."
[35] A pre-cursor to the Challenger League baseball, but in the town of Everett where they lived at the time.

August has Alex at Skull Island on the Cape with Skye, Aryzona, and Shawna, and their mom, playing miniature golf, and at Santa's Village in Jefferson, NH, with Santa. That same month they went to Clark's Trading Post in Lincoln, NH, where they printed a newspaper showing Alex on the front page, with the headline, 'Alex Gentile Captured by the Wolf Man', a character at the park. They also visited Elf University that month, where Alex got his 'Elf' diploma.

In September he had a big birthday party, where he's surrounded by all his friends, a literal mob of children, relatives, schoolmates, and neighbors. A few days later, he's at Paparazzi's, where the staff sang happy birthday to him.

That October they visit Rockingham Park to see the Halloween carved-pumpkin display. In November Penny, Jerry, and Alex were on MATV, Channel 15 in Malden being interviewed on what kinds of things Alex likes to do (it would fill a dozen scrapbooks). That Thanksgiving they were at the Holiday Shriners' Parade, where they gave Alex a Shriners' hat.

In December, Alex got a letter from the Boston Ballet, inviting him to the dress rehearsal for the Nutcracker Suite at the Colonial Theater, where he got to meet and have his picture taken with all the dancers. Later that month they went on the Polar Express train ride to the North Pole and to a Christmas party at the Malden Police department.

What a full schedule. What a wonderful life.

There's a 'Grammy' book, dedicated to Jerry's mother after she passed away, with some great shots of Alex and Esther, including the last pictures taken of them together.

There's a 'First Communion' book capturing this special event in Alex's life, which took place on May 8th, Mother's Day. Fitting, considering how important having Alex take communion was to Penny. It shows Alex at home getting ready, and at the church, with Skye helping him down the aisle. There's a great photo of Alex, Penny, and Jerry, with Father Bill Minnegan, and one of Alex sitting in the middle of the altar. There are pictures of the whole class, boys and girls, all in their white suits and gowns, and of Alex with Penny's parents, as well as some professionally done photos of Alex. There are pictures of the party afterward, with all Alex's family and friends. One of these has a very special place in the author's heart, the only picture of his wife, Kathy, and him, together with Alex.

135

There's another book with the theme, Making Memories, full of mixed snapshots of Alex from his first three or four years, with his therapist, Sandra, and all Penny's brother, Jimmy's, kids. There's also a special Birthday Book, with pictures of Alex from each birthday starting at year one and going to twenty-one, his last year.

There's a book of random pictures that Penny made in 2002, which includes her very first scrapping page, with Alex's first booboo, Alex at the Bunker Hill Day Parade, and at the Dorchester Day parade, and at the Stoneham Zoo, and the Liberty Bell in Philly, as well as the ice sculptures in Boston, and at the Gym and Swim[36] meet where volunteers from Tufts College worked with Special Needs kids.

In addition to the twelve books I've described, there are six more books with Disney themes, as well as a Sesame Place and a Special Olympics book, twenty-one in all, and counting. Penny is currently working on a Santa Claus book of all the pictures of Alex with Santa.

Penny has not only created a wonderful, loving tribute to Alex's memory, she has created a piece of art.

---

[36] Unfortunately, this program is no longer operating.

Chapter 25 – Alex Passes Over

Then one day, as quietly as he had slipped into this world, Alex slipped out of it. Alex died on the morning of June 9th, 2018. His father found him on the floor of his room. He had passed away during the night.

Penny and Jerry had to do everything for Alex. That kind of dependency builds a bond that can't be broken in this life, and when it is finally severed, in the end that all things must come to, it shatters the heart. Penny and Jerry had to face the worst of all adversities when Alex died. It took everyone, his teachers, his friends, his relatives, and teammates by surprise. No one expected it.

Penny's oldest brother, Jimmy was at his birth and his death.

"None of us felt that Alex would have a short life. He had never suffered seizures until just a few months before his death."

Marlene believed Alex's life expectancy wasn't good, but was sure he would outlive expectations.

Alex's neurologist told them his condition had no impact on his life expectancy. He wanted them to focus on helping Alex develop. He gave them hope.

It was certainly the last thing Penny and Jerry expected. On the contrary, they thought he would outlive them. In fact, they had gone to great lengths all through his life to find people who would act as guardians for Alex in the event of their deaths. They offered their house, if only the person or persons would promise to take care of Alex and not put him in an institution or hospital. Several people were asked. Not everyone agreed, and the good people who did agree, changed over time.

Jeff, Jimmy's oldest son, who is a physician and works in a hospital, is one of the people who was asked and agreed to be Alex's guardian. He promised to take him in as one of his own and make sure he never had to go into an institution (like Penny's sibling did). It meant a lot to them.

The scene at the hospital where Alex was taken was heart-wrenching and dramatic in the extreme.

Jimmy – "I was at the emergency room when Alex was brought out of the ambulance, and watched them work their hearts out to save this child (his voice breaks here), so many people working on him. It's the number one worst thing that can happen to a person is to lose a child. Their whole life was in this child!"

Jerry went berserk when they wouldn't let them see Alex. Some of his organs were being donated and he needed to be quarantined. Jerry threatened to break down the door and security was called, then the police.

Mary Gasdia is a longtime friend. Their kids were in Early Intervention together.

"Penny called and blurted out, 'Alex died!' She was hysterical. I dropped everything and rushed over to their house but no one was there."

She called Penny who told her they were at the hospital, and she drove right over.

She didn't know about Alex's seizures. They were busy seeing their oldest daughter off to China to work with the Chinese Olympic athletic department, and were completely surprised by his death.

"When I got there, it was a heartbreaking scene."

There were three police cars in the ER parking area with their lights flashing. She ran into the emergency room.

Mary - "Penny, Jerry, and four cops were standing in a circle. Jerry and one of the cops were screaming at each other. Penny was sobbing. I pushed my way into the circle and hugged Penny and Jerry. 'What's going on?' I asked."

They wouldn't let them be with Alex. It was against hospital policy. Alex's organs had been donated, and he had been taken to the morgue to wait for them to take him away. Jerry tried to kick the door in.

Mary - "I talked to the older cop, who was mad and yelling, and explained the situation. 'Their Special Needs son just died. He's never been alone. You need to let them be with him.' "

Penny and Jerry just wanted to sit outside the room where Alex's body was being kept. The hospital finally agreed and everyone calmed down. They were able to sit outside the morgue until they took Alex, although they had to leave and come back when another body was brought in.

Mary – "One of the younger cops went to Alex's wake."

Dana Brown, the principal said that Jerry was quite upset[37].

---

[37] Jerry, Penny, and Mary do not remember Dana being there, but under the circumstances he quite well could have been and not been noticed, or he may have

"One cop, the older one, wanted to arrest him for disturbing the peace. The other cop, the young one, asked him, 'What do you want? How can we help?' and was able to help calm him down."

As with the lack of diagnosis and misdiagnosis early in Alex's life, the cause of his death was difficult to determine. It took several months and multiple attempts. Apparently, Alex started having the seizures a year before he died. They became more frequent during his final months. They called them Rett episodes.

Dana – "We knew when Alex wasn't having a great day."

But sometimes appearances can be deceiving, especially with someone like Alex.

Jimmy – "On his last day Alex was having a fantastic day. There was no indication he was not well. It never occurred to any of us that there was something wrong."

Alex may have died of sleep apnea.

Jimmy – "They were told recently that Alex had sleep apnea. If they had known earlier, perhaps they would have started sleeping with him."

John and Sheila thought Alex would live forever. They had no idea he would die young.

Sheila – "The kids were devastated when they heard he had died."

John and Sheila got an early morning call from Penny and Jerry and knew something was terribly wrong.

John – "We knew it was bad news."

Sheila – "He was a big part of everyone's life. There's an empty feeling now that he is gone."

Penny and Jerry were told little. They are still in the dark, although as was seen in Chapter 6, this is not that unusual in these cases. Alex seemed to beat the odds, until the last moment.

Paula, Penny's neighbor – "Over the past few months, I noticed Alex was going to the hospital about three times a month. It was awful. He always came back and was fine. And every time he came home I'd run over to make sure he was OK. Then, one day he just didn't come home (cries)."

Paula believes special needs children are gifts from God.

Paula – "The word special isn't in there for nothing. It takes a special kind of person to be able to properly take care of them. I've

---

heard the story, but it rings true and points to the restraint the police showed.

never seen anybody do it as Penny and Jerry have. It still blows my mind."

Jimmy – "Alex wouldn't have lived half as long without Penny and Jerry's care, love, and support, although I didn't think Alex had a short life-expectancy."

Like his birth, his death was a mystery. Jerry told me that the final and third report from the coroner found the cause of Alex's death to be complications from MECP2.

The wake and funeral were sad, but joyful, for the turnout was beyond expectations. The whole town of Malden came to pay their respects. Hundreds waited in line to see his casket, which was open. He looked so small. Uncle Jimmy and Aunt Marlene were there together with their spouses. They were both with Penny and Jerry to lend their support from the day Alex died throughout their ordeal. Penny's dad was also at the wake, sitting in the front row, watching over his little grandson. Penny's brother Joe was there with his wife, son, and four girls[38]. It was touching to see Alex's young cousins deal with his passing.

The mayor, Gary Christenson, and the principal, Dana Brown, were there, as were countless team members, special and typical schoolmates, girlfriends, teachers, and strangers, all there to pay their respects to this young man who had so little but gave so much.

A video played in the next room with an endless loop of pictures of Alex chronicling his life from his birth to the most recent days. It was a stunning, captivating, and incredibly moving display. Many of the pictures were from Penny's scrapbooks.

Several kids from the high school sports teams, who had played with Alex in Unified Sports, were there, many of them young athletes of color. It made me proud of this small New England city, its schools, and its young people.

A long line of people trailed out the door throughout the day and evening. At the end of the night, Jerry stood over Alex's casket, holding his son gently, as if comforting him.

Dave Bugden and his wife, Lisa, who had flown up from Florida in the middle of their hectic schedules, were there, sharing Penny and Jerry's grief as they had shared their joy with Alex in Disney World.

---

[38] Joe has a wonderful family. His daughters are Emma, Hayley, and the twins, Abigail and Kathleen. His son's name is Joseph.

At the funeral the next day, the church was packed. All of us should be so lucky to go out with such a bang, with such a show of respect and love as Alex did.

Sheila and John called their daughter Annabelle in New York City that morning and told her about Alex. They told the kids later that day. All of them went to his funeral. Annabelle worked late the night before in New York, and then drove all night to be there the next day for the funeral, for Penny and Jerry.

It was a beautiful ceremony and a tribute to his parents' continuing love and devotion, with music and prayers, people kneeling and standing. Alex would have enjoyed it immensely. Who knows, maybe he did.

Paula's daughter, Hannah, played guitar and sang a beautiful rendition of Alleluia. There wasn't a dry eye in the house.

Paula — "She had a hard time at the funeral when she was supposed to sing. She was bawling her eyes out right up to the time to sing. And my daughter is very private. She doesn't show her emotions normally, but that day she was extremely emotional. She said, 'I don't know if I can do it, Mom', but I told her, you can do it, you're a professional, and she did. When the time came, she sang it perfectly. She did a great job for Alex."

The priest's sermon was strong, urging Penny and Jerry to go on despite their anguish, and praising what they had done. Dana also spoke, as did Paula, both very eloquently, in tribute to Alex[39] and his parents.

The drive to the cemetery was over eight miles and very long, with dozens of cars, stopping traffic in two cities and on Route 1. One of the most poignant moments was when the funeral procession passed by Malden High. There, standing in front of the school, were hundreds of kids. It looked like the entire Student body had come out to pay their respect, all races and colors, all his schoolmates. It was one of the most inspiring, touching sights you could picture, like seeing a rainbow on a stormy day. Can you imagine how it must have affected Penny and Jerry, to see such a tribute to their son? Despite their anguish, it must have made them smile inside with pride and joy.

Alex's passing was felt by all.

---

[39] See Chapters 27 and 28.

Dana - "The Special Ed program director called me after Alex went by and told me people there weren't doing so well. It was so emotional to be standing out there that they needed support afterwards. They had to talk to the kids and the adults."

Alex's tributes didn't stop there.

Despite the sad occasion, Dana told me he almost had to laugh at the wake when he saw many of the flowers were from some of the restaurants like Kelly's and Kowloon. It only went to prove that Alex was a celebrity in Malden, the city where he lived, and how much he was part of things, the holiday parades, Challenger League baseball, the Special Olympics, and more.

Dana – "Wherever they were with Alex, it was an event."

Those who know them and have seen what Jerry and Penny did with Alex cannot express their admiration enough. So it was hard at the cemetery to watch them put their young son in the ground. At the end Penny embraced the coffin sobbing. It was heart-rending, yet beautiful, the last painful expression of her grief before she left him forever.

Both Penny and Jerry have been ennobled by their deeds, not because Alex died, but because he lived so fully. They made it so and that should give them great joy and pride, in themselves and in Alex, and turn their tears of sadness into tears of happiness.

Dana – "It's an exceptional story, because of Penny and Jerry. I know they may not realize it now, when they are beating themselves up and are angry, but I hope they come to realize how special they are. After thirty-eight years in education, I have never seen anything as wonderful as how they took care of and supported Alex. I've never seen anything like that kind of unconditional love and support."

As sad as it seems, Alex's life is a story of joy and happiness, of how love can overcome all odds and a boy with so little can make such a difference in so many people's lives. These thoughts can help sustain us, and will remain with us, as we all move forward thru life.

Chapter 26 – Alex's Legacy

Alex left a lasting legacy. It was more than his friendly personality and shy smile that attracted people to him.

Dana Brown, Principal of Malden High – "It was like it was planned, Alex going through grade school and graduating from high school at eighteen, and he stayed on (he was still going to Malden High when he died). Special Olympic Day Games, Unified Sports, Challenger League baseball, the new renovations with accommodations for Special Needs classrooms, it all happened during Alex's lifetime in the Malden Public Schools. It's almost like he was teaching us. That to me is not a coincidence. It could not have been written better. A lot of this will be Alex's Legacy."

The Malden Special Olympics will be named after Alex (see Chapter 29), and Forestdale Park, where Alex played baseball, will be renamed to 'Alex Gentile Memorial Park' in his honor on opening day in April of 2019. There is also the Alex Gentile Scholarship fund, which is being set up by his family and friends. A portion of the proceeds from this book will be donated to this fund, which is for scholarships for those wanting to go into Special Education or work with disabled persons.

Jimmy, Penny's older brother – "You could see the determination in Alex's face when he tried something."

Jim coached sports for twenty years and had seen determination in a lot of faces. He recognized it in Alex's face.

Jimmy – "He was able to do everything he wanted to do. If he had been a normal kid, he would have been a star athlete because of his determination."

Jim insists that Alex taught them all a lot. Penny and Jerry were determined to not let their child be left out, but to make sure he led a full life. They never allowed him to go without.

Jimmy feels bad. He took Alex for granted. He thought he would always be there. He wasn't as close to Alex as he could have been due to his demanding job at Boston Edison, busy and concerned with his own family. He retired in 2004 and in thirty-eight years there were only eight weeks when he didn't work over forty hours, but that was nothing to what Penny and Jerry did.

Jimmy – "Their life was 24/7 taking care of Alex, not one minute was he ever neglected or left alone. No matter what obstacles they faced, Penny and Jerry were going to succeed, never woe is me or feeling sorry for themselves."

Jimmy couldn't stress enough the support Alex got from Jerry's mother. He is not the only person to say so.

Jimmy – "She was special, the most supportive person you could ask for."

Dana – "I've seen school systems, even things at Malden, where it's not the right way to treat human beings, but the first couple of times we had Special Olympic Day Games, it was the one event each year where we had the most number of student volunteers sign up to help. A lot of kids, if you talk to them now after ten or fifteen years, if you ask them about that experience that caused them to be a Special Ed teacher, or caused them to go into education, or made them volunteer at the hospital, or made them see Special Needs people like everyone else, Alex was at the center of it. He benefited along with his parents, but the growth and support of everybody around them was tremendous."

Penny and Jerry are carrying on Alex's legacy, championing him now that he's gone, as they did when he was here with us. They are the poster children for parents of Special Needs kids, the model which we might all try to follow. If you ask them, though, they will tell you they didn't do anything special. They just did what they needed to do to take care of their boy. Courage is the kind of thing that often springs up unnoticed after the thing is done.

Penny and Jerry were invited to Wheelock College twice to talk about Individual Educational Planning (IEP) to groups of future Special Ed teachers. They asked the audience, the teachers, "When you go into an IEP, who do you represent?"

They answered, "The student."

"No," Jerry replied. "You represent the administration. Everything is controlled by them." Jerry told them that this is their first ethical challenge, where theory meets reality. "It's all a game," said Jerry. "You need to know how to play. The parents are the boss."

You have to be engaged to make this happen and stand up for your rights and the rights of your students. You must be informed.

Dana – "As an educator, sometimes you have to forget about rules and administration and lawyers and 'by the book'. Sometimes you have to be creative. Sometimes what's needed is not in the book."

The support Alex had changed his life, but he changed ours as well. Alex inspired people like Skye MacDonald and Alyssa Figueiredo, to go on and help others with special needs.

The Alex Gentile Memorial Scholarship Fund will also remind people of Alex's gift to us. The criteria to apply for the scholarship are that you are a student going to school for Special Ed or to work with people with disabilities.

Alex touched so many people.

Paula – "There's a reason for this. Special Needs children touch people's lives. They just do, if they are open. Alex always made us smile."

On the eighth of November, 2018, Alex's parents and friends held a fund raiser for the Alex Gentile Memorial Scholarship (see Chapter 29). At the ceremony, Barbara Scibelli, the school's administrator and a leading force behind the Special Olympic Day Games, read a letter from the school's principal, Chris Mastrangelo. After apologizing for not being able to attend, the letter continues:

> *"I think it is fitting that this is a night of laughter, because Alex's smile was so infectious. Who would have ever guessed that he would have brought so much joy to the lives of so many.*
>
> *"Whether it was at one of the many MHS events that Alex attended or just simply having lunch in the café, Alex always seemed to be the 'life of the party'. There was, however, one event that he seemed to truly 'own'. That was the Malden Special Olympics. It started with TEAM ALEX, a group of family, friends, and staff that rallied around Alex during the games. It certainly appears that this day was the highlight of the year for Alex and all who loved him.*
>
> *"It is in that spirit that I am proud to announce that the Malden Special Olympics will now be know as 'THE ALEX GAMES'. It makes sense, let's be honest, on that day it was Alex's world and the rest of us just lived in it. This will allow his spirit to shine on that day for years to come."*
>
> *Sincerely,*
>
> *Chris Mastrangelo*

Chapter 27 – Dana Brown's Funeral Oration: 'Alex'

Alex…there was, and is, no need to say his last name. Alex.

I had the honor and pleasure of being Alex's Principal at Malden High School. For many of us at the school, he was, well, just Alex. We knew of Alex before he got to Malden High School and when he got there…watch out! He was in many ways bigger than life; a Rock Star!

Part of Alex's legacy will be the profound impact he had on the Malden Public Schools, Malden High School in particular, the caring and dedicated staff there, and most importantly, the other students. The Malden Public Schools now thinks differently about how they work with special needs students and their families. Alex and his mom and dad helped lead this change.

As I had a chance to reflect on Alex's life, it all started to make sense to me; Alex's legacy…it must have been part of God's plan, with Alex's at the center. God does work in mysterious ways.

How else to explain that as Alex became part of the Malden Public Schools, Malden High School just happened to be undergoing a 77 million dollar renovation, ensuring that students of all abilities would have access to first class spaces to learn, to work, to play, and to participate in physical therapy. The new spaces certainly benefited Alex as well as countless others.

What about Malden's own Special Olympic Day Games? They were founded just as Alex and his parents seemed to most need them in his life. Team Alex was formed and became a formidable and courageous group of students and adults, dedicated to making Alex's Olympic experiences special, year after year. Alex's team accomplished that and more. When they paraded into Macdonald Stadium, you knew they were there with Alex at the center. I get goose bumps thinking about the parade of champions with Alex leading the way.

And then this…not long after Alex entered Malden High School the Unified Sports Program was started, putting students of all abilities into the same gym, playing all types of sports and games together. The same athletes that Alex cheered for at night were now at his side playing together with him during the day.

And boy did Alex get excited cheering for Malden High School. At Malden High School and in the community, Alex was known everywhere. Band and choral concerts, football and basketball games and other school events; you always knew Alex was there.

Of course, Alex and I had our own special bond; we played this cat and mouse game each morning, with Alex tilting his head down, looking away and smirking, making sure I would call his name loudly to get his attention. I insisted that he look at me and smile. His head would turn slowly, the smirk turned into a great big smile, my morning made. My days were always more complete when I got to greet Alex. There were other Malden High School faculty and students, too numerous to mention, who had their own special bond with Alex. He deserved and received special care from many. I do need to give a special shout out to the Class of 2015, Alex's class.

It wasn't always fun; a few years ago a school committee member became concerned with the traffic flow behind the cafeteria of the high school. Specifically, the cars, vans, and buses that transported our special education students were creating traffic jams each morning. The proposed solution was to send the special education students to the entrance at Route 60 behind the auto shop. Imagine me having to tell Penny that Alex was going to have to be dropped off at Route 60 behind the school, an elevator ride and two long hallways away from his morning destination. The thought still gives me agita...Alex was never, ever going to have to 'settle' in his lifetime. 'Alex 96' was going to park wherever it wanted to, and I wasn't about to tell Penny otherwise!

Speaking of Penny and Jerry...I would be remiss if I didn't pay special tribute to two people here today that lost the center of their world, their Alex. When we speak about the triumphs and victories that Alex experienced, we have to speak first about Penny and Jerry, two selfless, courageous, and loving parents, unmatched in many ways. The joy and glory Alex brought to our lives was not without some pain and suffering for Penny and Jerry. Without the lives of Penny and Jerry, there is no wonderful life of Alex. Without their unconditional love and sacrifice, there is no lasting legacy for Alex. I also want to gently remind my friends that they were the center of each other's lives before there was Alex.

I want to challenge each and everyone of us in the church today to keep the legacy of Alex alive; volunteer at the Special Olympics...donate to a summer camp...or an after-school program that works with students of differing abilities...call or visit Penny or

Jerry. Alex would approve of any of these. From above, he'll tilt his head, smirk, and then break open wide his great big smile.

Chapter 28 – Paula English's Funeral Oration: If There is Ever a Day When We Can't be Together

"If there ever comes a day when we can't be together.
Keep me in your heart, I'll be there forever."

This is a Pooh bear quote, Alex's favorite Disney character.

I have been blessed and honored to know this amazing family for 19 years. It has been the past 6 years that we have bonded, because they were there, their presence was so dominant, and in a moment I'll get to that...There are no words that I can begin to say, that could possibly express the loss of this beautiful and amazing young man.

On Saturday when I learned of his passing, the only words I could say to my dear friend Penny were, I cannot tell you, I know how you feel, but what I can tell you is you and Jerry were the best parents any child could ask for.

This amazing young man, who had the most infectious smile, lived an amazing life. So Jerry and Penny, I know nothing I say will ever take your pain away, my dear friends, but please carry on, with no regret because you gave your child an amazing life.

Six years ago this week the city of Malden experienced something that never happened (before), the Malden High School girls softball team went to the State finals, and Alex, Penny, and Jerry were there every step of the way.

Penny and Jerry were Alex's feet, Alex's voice. I will stand with them both and be their feet, their voice. I am asking you all today, please let us not let go of the legacy of this young man. Let us carry his name in a way he deserves to be remembered...it is my plan in the next few months to start a fundraiser to initiate a scholarship in the name of this precious young man. I ask you all to help me keep his legacy alive, please stand with me to help his amazing parents get through each day...let us not go silently to Jerry and Penny...

Chapter 29 – The Scholarship Foundation Fundraiser

On Nov 8th, 2018, Penny and Jerry put on a fundraiser for the Alex Gentile Memorial Scholarship Fund for Special Education. Their dear friend and neighbor, Paula English, who has some experience in these things, suggested and produced the event. Alex's friends, Alyssa Figueiredo and Samantha French, helped organize things. It was held at Mixx 360 at 665 Broadway in Malden, and was a phenomenal success by any standard, just spectacular.

Gary Christianson, the mayor of Malden gave the following introduction to the event.

The Malden community is still coming to grips on the loss of Alex, but based on the outpouring of support to his parents, Penny and Jerry, I am certain that Alex will never be forgotten. From the first annual scholarship fundraiser in his name where there was standing room only, to different school events like the MHS Band Winter Concert and Play Pro's Fall Play dedications to Alex, it has been heartwarming to see everyone come together to remember the positive impact he had on the Malden Public Schools and the city in general. And we are not done yet, as over the winter Councilor Barbara Murphy and I are teaming up to make Forestdale Park, which is home to the Challenger League of which Alex was a dedicated player, into the Alex Gentile Park. As they say, "anyone can catch your eye, but it takes someone special to catch your heart." Alex captured all of our hearts and will long be remembered!

The list of entertainers included singers Gary Cherone's 'Hurtsmile' and Diane Ellis, as well as Hannah Calderone. Comedians Paul Gilligan, Dave Russo, and Bob Gautreau tore up the house with laughter. The DJ for the night was Chris Fiore. All the entertainers donated their time and fine talents to the event. It was not only a rousing good time, promoting a wonderful cause, it was an amazing tribute to Alex and his parents.

Over 300 folks attended, including many of the people in this book. Besides Gary Christenson, the mayor, Dana Brown was there, along with Barbara Scibelli, as were Penny's brothers Jimmy and Joe, and her sister Marlene. Bobbi Jo and her incredible daughters, Skye, Aryzona, and Shawna were there, along with John and Sheila

Krupcheck and their children. Paul and Cindy Kelloway, Samantha French and Alyssa Figueiredo, Mary Gasdia and Alex's friends from Challenger League also attended, and so many others. The author and his wife, Kathy, were there, of course.

The food was donated by Anthony DeCotis, the owner of Mixx 360, as was the room, which I can attest was first-rate. Alex would have loved the cake. There were dozens of gift baskets, a table full of them, donated by local businesses and neighbors, family and friends, to be raffled off as gifts to the lucky ticket holders – tickets for sports events like Red Sox and Bruins games, movies and shows, concerts and gift certificates to restaurants, and more.

A special surprise was the Malden High School Marching Band playing outside by the door. The kids insisted on being there and playing. It was really stunning.

Over $6000 was raised that night to add to the $10,000 already collected, all given in the name of a very incredible boy, Alex Gentile. His legacy will live on in the lives of those children who are helped by the recipients of his scholarship.

Chapter 30 – Conclusions

No one can know the depth of grief and loss Penny and Jerry must feel at the death of their son. He was everything to them, everything. Their reason to be seems gone without him, their life, empty. As they did at his birth, however, when they faced difficulty and uncertainty, they met his death bravely, head on. Despite their terrible pain, they have carried on and turned their tears of grief into tears of joy and pride. Pride in Alex and his indomitable will, his smile that made all dark days bright. Pride in his teachers and peers for making Alex a part of their lives, and theirs a part of his. Their lives have been enriched and they have grown by knowing him.

Those young people and athletes who included him in their lives, felt better for it. Those who taught him and were challenged by him grew in the process. As they strived to change his life for the better, they were bettered. As they got to know Alex and appreciate his special needs, they learned about themselves, how to smile, enjoy life, and be grateful for what they had.

Penny and Jerry can be proud, as well, for their selfless love and courage, for making his every day a day of happiness, a day full of love. As Paula said, no child could have been loved more. In the terrible test and joyous task they were given, they have won. They nailed it! In my eyes, they have been ennobled through their triumph in overcoming adversity. They are my heroes.

Neither of them thinks they did anything special, or feels they had to overcome great obstacles. There was no real drama in their lives or life-threatening events, although there were some scary moments. They just continued doing what they had been doing since Alex was born, taking him wherever they went. It was a routine, and that made it all seem easy.

I asked them if they had any advice for those in a similar situation and they told me, never give up, take it one day at a time, and give your child the best you can.

Penny – "Seeing Alex's face every morning when I woke up, was all the motivation I needed."

Penny and Jerry taught me that love can blind one to difficulty, hardship, cost, and disabilities. Love can overcome all. That courage comes from not seeing or considering what could or is happening to you, but only in what you are doing to save those you love.

The people around Alex, his friends and teachers, paras and sitters, coaches and teammates, are extraordinarily giving people, with open hearts, full of kindness. These are the ones that really make Alex's story special.

Alex was special in another way, as well. At twenty-one, Alex, in my eyes, was sinless. He was as innocent as a newborn babe, without guilt. How many of us can say that?

Alex lived in the moment. He didn't dwell on past regrets or misfortunes. He didn't worry about future trials or troubles. He simply lived, totally in the present moment. Some would say that is the definition of enlightenment.

This is not a sad story, but a joyous one. It is not his death and our loss we should be mourning, but his life and spirit we should be celebrating. If we celebrate with tears, that is OK, too, because they will be tears of happiness and gratitude for having known him. Life is a gift. Alex proved that. All those in this book, especially Penny and Jerry, can be grateful and proud, for Alex was a child of God and they have done God's will, by treating him with such love and kindness.

Though it is hard, Penny and Jerry are now showing that same courage that made Alex's life so special. Their lives continue. Although they keep themselves busy with work and friends, they take time each day to remember Alex. They visit his gravesite, bringing flowers and balloons. They water the grass and flowers on hot days and talk to him. On his 22nd birthday, they brought presents and more balloons. Several of their friends and neighbors were there as well to help celebrate.

Penny has quit her job of thirty-years to work at the high school with Special Needs kids, helping other children just like she did Alex. Aiding in the writing and promotion of this book is another way they plan to move forward and keep Alex's legacy alive. To Penny and Jerry, their Alex was as good as anybody, the star athlete or the brilliant scholar. With that kind of attitude, no wonder it seemed easy for them.

Those who knew Alex at Malden High still go to classes and participate in Unified Sports. His teammates in Challenger League baseball still play every week in the spring at the field - though it's now the Alex Gentile Memorial Park. The Special Olympics - now also renamed after Alex - still takes place every May, and although there is no Team Alex, parents and friends still cheer and clap. Alex is still there, in spirit. For all who knew him carry Alex in their hearts. He still makes them smile.

Author's Note

I met Jerry in the mid-1980s through our mutual friends, Paul and Cindy Kelloway, when they lived in Gloucester. Cindy and another good friend, Dave Bugden, worked at Malden Trust with Jerry. Paul and Cindy are long-time friends of my wife, Kathy, and me. Jerry was one of the gang and an ardent music fan, often getting concert tickets for us. We were all intrigued one weekend when Jerry brought a young lady to the beach house and introduced her to the group.

"This is Penny," he announced.

She fit right in and we've been friends ever since.

I remember when Alex was born, and knew how much Penny had wanted a baby and the trouble she had already gone through. We were all very happy for them. Then we learned about Alex's condition.

I, like some, felt badly for them. It sounded like their lives would be very difficult, taking care of such a disabled child. Penny and Jerry didn't seem to be fazed. Like everything, Jerry took it in stride, one day at a time. He even continued going to concerts, which was one of his great passions.

The first time I remember seeing Alex was at one of his birthday parties at their apartment in Everett, perhaps his first. I really didn't pay a lot of attention to Alex. At that young age, he looked like any typical cute kid, although it was obvious that Penny and Jerry loved him very much.

I went to a good percentage of his birthday parties over the years, and Penny and Jerry would take Alex with them when visiting our mutual friends in Gloucester, or to meet us at the Bisuteki restaurant for dinner. Alex was just part of the gang.

I'd always said "Hi, big guy," to Alex, and Jerry would always say, "Smile for Joe". Sometimes Alex would give a shy smile, sometimes he wouldn't, and that would be that.

Penny and Jerry more than made up for my lack of attention, especially the birthday parties, which were lavish, always something different, always dozens of kids. I seldom talked to anybody, other than a quick hello, and would end up observing Alex.

Seeing all the typical kids jumping around and yelling each year at his parties as he grew older, made me feel sorry for him, because he couldn't walk or talk. Even his friends from the Special Needs class seemed to be developing faster than Alex. But I had to smile when I

155

saw how happy he was, and how he was always the center of attention, especially when his girlfriends surrounded him. Then I had to laugh.

Right from the beginning I was extremely impressed by how Penny and Jerry took care of him. One of the few people at Alex's parties I talked to were Penny's dad, Reggio, and her brother, Joey, both of whom used to sit around like me. I remember them both expressing some sadness about Alex, feeling sorry for Penny, like I did. But I realized something and told them, "There couldn't be a child in the world more loved than Alex." After that, I never felt bad for them again. I thought Alex and his parents were just the greatest.

I took the liberty of putting the medium in the beginning of the book, although it took place a month after Alex's passing. Penny and Jerry have gone back several times since then. They taped the first session and played it for me. There's something uncanny in the way the medium seemed to pick up on things. As I transcribed it for the book, it seemed to me almost like a prophecy, so I put it in chapter 1. If you read that chapter again, you'll see what I'm talking about.

I was shocked when Alex died. Jerry called us that Saturday. My wife, Kathy, answered and stood mute with the phone in her hand afterward. We went to see them the next day. No one was there, so we sat and waited. Cindy Kelloway, our mutual friend, was there. Paula English, their next-door neighbor also came over. We were all feeling pretty badly. Cindy knew about Jerry's melt down at the hospital. Then Penny and Jerry returned home from the funeral home. Jimmy and Marlene were with them. Jimmy was driving.

Penny sat in the seat sobbing. It was heartrending. We all went over to comfort her. I went to Jerry. He looked at me in such distress. I wanted to help him somehow, but didn't know what to say. Then I hugged him and said, "We'll write a book."

A Poem by Kathy Bebo:

Alex was all sweetness
And smiles,
Loving you back
All the while.
This very special person,
I will never forget
We are so grateful
To have met.

Acknowledgements

This book could not have been written without the help of the wonderful people who told me their stories about Alex. They are the real authors of this book. These people not only helped Alex through his life as teachers, administrators, schoolmates, neighbors, relatives, and friends, but have helped keep Alex's legacy alive. I am forever indebted to these folks for their kind assistance and trust.

They are, in alphabetical order: Dana Brown, Gary Christianson, Bernie Colbert, Paula English, Alyssa Figueiredo, Marlene Fitzpatrick, Samantha French, Dawn Frim, Mary Gazdia, Ron Giovino, Rachel Hanlon, Cindy Kelloway, John and Sheila Krupcheck, Ryan LaRouche, Skye, Aryzona, and Shawna MacDonald, Jim Randazza, Marie Shea, and of course, Penny and Jerry Gentile. All were instrumental in the writing of this book.

Not only did Penny and Jerry share all their stories with me, but Penny provided her wonderful journal for the first chapters, and all her pictures. They also selected and arranged all the interviews. Even though they didn't want their names on the cover, they are the co-writers of this book and deserve a lot of the credit for it. Special thanks also to Dana Brown and Paula English for letting me include their funeral orations. After hearing them talk that day, I realized I could never give Alex a better tribute than they did. They said it all. I'm only echoing their words.

Like some, I had taken Alex for granted. I didn't realize until I started working on this book what a wonderful story it really is. So I thank Penny and Jerry and all their friends and family for sharing it with me, so that I can tell it to you.

Figure 18 - The Quit, a patchwork of Alex's life made out of his clothes

About the Author

Joe Bebo has nine full-length fiction books on Amazon, ranging from historical fiction and adventure, to science based thrillers and horror. He also has a non-fiction story about his summer playing drums with the Van Morrison Controversy band in 1968. Joe lives with his wife, Kathy, in Hudson, Massachusetts.

Made in the USA
Middletown, DE
03 May 2019